FRENCH
EIGHTEENTH-CENTURY
CLOCKS AND BAROMETERS

in the Wallace Collection

FRENCH
EIGHTEENTH-CENTURY

CLOCKS AND BAROMETERS

in the Wallace Collection

PETER HUGHES

**THE TRUSTEES OF
THE WALLACE COLLECTION
LONDON**

Copyright © 1994
Text: *The Trustees of the Wallace Collection*
Photographs: *The Trustees of the Wallace Collection,*
unless otherwise stated. All other photographs are
also copyright and were supplied by the sources
given in the photographic acknowledgements at the
back of the book.
Illustrations: *David Penney*

Published by The Trustees of the Wallace Collection,
Hertford House, Manchester Square,
London W1M 6BN, England

Book packaged by John Adamson
Designed by Chris Jones
Prepress by DawkinsColour
Printed by Balding + Mansell, Meridian House PLC

Set in Garamond and printed on Job Parilux matt
150 gsm with sponsorship by Job Parilux, Toulouse

ISBN 0 900785 45 4
British Library Cataloguing-in-Publication Data.
A catalogue record for this book is available from
the British Library.

All Rights Reserved. No part of this publication may be
reproduced or transmitted in any form or by any means, electronic
or mechanical, including photocopy, recording or any other
information storage and retrieval system, without prior permission
in writing from the publisher.

DEDICATION

FRENCH EIGHTEENTH-CENTURY
CLOCKS AND BAROMETERS
IN THE WALLACE COLLECTION
is published in memory of
Patrick John Hamilton
1936–1993

Patrick Hamilton had long been a cherished and valued friend of the Wallace Collection when, in November 1992, he was appointed a Trustee. He was then Director of Refining and Supply at Total Oil Great Britain and had already fostered Total's support of the Wallace Collection which, happily, still continues.

Born in Paris, Patrick Hamilton was a dedicated student of eighteenth-century France, an interest he acquired while at Brasenose College, Oxford. His absorbing passion was Sèvres porcelain (he became an expert in Sèvres bird painting of the 1750s and 1760s) and he was fascinated by the clocks in the Wallace Collection (especially the astronomical clock, see pp. 44–5, which he saw running again after conservation in 1991). His fondness for the Collection also extended to the staff who always welcomed his encouragement and enthusiasm.

Patrick Hamilton longed to inspire a wider audience to enjoy the Wallace Collection; we hope his wish will begin to be fulfilled by *French eighteenth-century clocks and barometers in the Wallace Collection*, the first in a series on aspects of this very special national museum. We are particularly grateful to his widow Caroline, his family, friends and colleagues at Total who have generously borne the costs of this publication so that we can all share Patrick Hamilton's admiration for these spectacular timepieces of the eighteenth century.

Rosalind Savill,
Director, The Wallace Collection.

CONTENTS

FOREWORD

The clocks and barometers in this book were nearly all acquired by
Richard Seymour-Conway (1800–70), 4th Marquess of Hertford.
Lord Hertford was the principal collector behind the formation of
the Wallace Collection and the father of Sir Richard Wallace, whose
widow bequeathed it to the British nation in 1897. He acquired the
clocks as examples of French eighteenth-century furniture, rather
than as horological masterpieces; indeed several of them form part of
much larger pieces of furniture, such as wardrobes and filing-
cabinets (see pp. 22–5, 36–7 and 52–3). Two clocks (see pp. 18–19
and 54–5) were acquired by the 3rd Marquess of Hertford, one as
early as 1802, and passed to the 4th Marquess by descent. These two,
together with nine other clocks and four of the barometers, were in
Hertford House at the time of Lord Hertford's death in August
1870, while the other twenty-five clocks and one barometer were in
his Parisian apartments at no. 2 rue Laffitte and nos. 3 and 5 rue
Taitbout. Most of Lord Hertford's clocks were thus in Paris and,
since he lived most of his life there, the ones from his Parisian
apartments are those he would have known best. There were,
nevertheless, some outstanding French clocks among those
inventoried at Hertford House in 1870, including the great
astronomical clock (pp. 44–5) acquired at the Stowe sale of 1848.
Since clock movements have often been altered by later clockmakers,
some of the alterations to the clock movements are French work of
the nineteenth century, while others are English work and the same
applies to the barometers. These alterations are most unlikely to
have been carried out for Lord Hertford and were probably made for
the previous owners from whom he acquired them. After Lord
Hertford's death the clocks from his Parisian collection were
brought over to London by Sir Richard Wallace, who lent many of
them to the Bethnal Green Museum between 1872 and 1875, before
incorporating them, with the clocks from Lord Hertford's London
collection, in the furnishings of Hertford House.

CLOCK CASES IN EIGHTEENTH-CENTURY FRANCE

Eighteenth-century French clockmakers did not make their clock cases, but confined themselves to making the movements. This division of labour resulted from the traditional guild system, which, though subject to certain loopholes, was still in force in eighteenth-century Paris. It is thus an absurdity to illustrate a clock from this period in a book and attribute the whole clock in a caption to the craftsman whose name appears on the dial, particularly since the cases were generally more costly than the movements. The clockmaker might of course commission a clock case from other craftsmen; he was a member of a relatively wealthy guild and was often involved in the retailing of clocks. The production of an eighteenth-century clock case would have involved several different craftsmen. A cabinet-made case would have been made by a cabinetmaker, but with the bronze mounts cast by a founder and chased and gilded by a gilder on metal; elaborate mounts would have been cast from an original model provided by a sculptor. The clock dial, supplied by the clockmaker with the movement, would, in the early eighteenth century, have been cast by a founder and then chased and gilded by a gilder on metal, while the enamel numbers, inserted individually, would have been painted and fired by an enameller; in the

later eighteenth century the whole dial would have been painted and fired by the enameller. With a gilt-bronze case, a sculptor would have provided the original model to be cast by a founder and chased and gilded by a gilder. Louis XVI gilt-bronze clock cases are often supported on marble plinths, supplied by a *marbrier*. An eighteenth-century clock case was thus a work of collaboration; even dominant artistic personalities like André-Charles Boulle or Charles Cressent would have entrusted much of the execution of their clock cases to other hands.

The influence of André-Charles Boulle on the French eighteenth-century clock case can hardly be exaggerated, since it was he who gave early eighteenth-century clocks much of their sculptural and allegorical character. The late seventeenth-century clock case had generally been shaped like a rectangular box, sometimes with a domed or arched hood and often with a glass panel at the front to show the beat of the pendulum. At the end of the seventeenth century Boulle designed an hour-glass-shaped case for his celebrated Love Triumphing over Time model (see pp. 18–19 and 30–1), adopting a theme which was to be

Love Triumphing over Time clock c. 1712– c. 1720 (detail)

taken up in numerous later clock cases. The same model shows the prominence of gilt-bronze mounts in Boulle's work; this is partly due to the freedom from guild regulations enjoyed by his workshop in the Louvre. Boulle often bought the sculptural models for his figurative mounts from such prominent sculptors as Girardon or the Coustou

Venus clock c. 1715

brothers, but he himself also conceived clock cases in sculptural terms. This can be seen with three of the models listed in his 1715 Act of Renunciation, by which he made over his workshop to his four sons in return for an annuity: on the Venus clock (pp. 20–1) the Venus and Cupid are taller than the case containing the movement, and on the Three Fates clock (pp. 22–3) and the wardrobe clock (pp. 24–5) the dial is set within a gilt-bronze cartouche encircled by allegorical figures. This use of large-scale figures, cast in the round, anticipates many Louis XVI clock designs; in the transitional period between the Louis XV and Louis XVI styles Boulle's figurative clock designs were occasionally revived in early neo-classical forms (see pp. 76–7). His most sumptuous and sophisticated clock case design is, however, his Four Continents clock (pp. 28–9), where the term figures remain firmly attached to the case, but on which the lines of the pedestal lead the eye up into the clock case above, unlike the richer version of his Love Triumphing over Time model (pp. 18–19), in which clock and pedestal are two separate entities.

The sculptural treatment of clock cases continued during the early years of Louis XV's reign. The *pendule aux biches*, or clock with does (pp. 34–5), recently attributed to Bernard I Van Risamburgh, not only has a curvilinear case with the corner uprights angled diagonally outwards, but actually rests on the backs of four gracefully modelled gilt-bronze does, who gaze upwards at Diana in her chariot. Still more sculptural are the clocks of Charles Cressent, who had trained as a sculptor under his father, François Cressent. The Diana and accompanying child and animals on his filing cabinet clock of 1740–5 (pp. 36–7) are perhaps the finest figurative mounts in the Wallace Collection, being both graceful and intensely lifelike, though Cressent had already used the Diana figure, without the goddess's attributes, cn a slightly earlier Boulle marquetry bracket clock at Waddesdon Manor. Cressent was also one of the first makers of gilt-bronze cartel clocks, in which the clock and bracket of earlier wall clocks were ellided into one

gilt-bronze unit, called a cartel from the word given to a type of decorative wall cartouche. The Cressent cartel clock in the Wallace Collection (pp. 42–3) takes up the Love Triumphing over Time theme from André-Charles Boulle, while enriching it with picturesque detail such as the rocks with snails crawling over them beneath Father Time, poetically described by Cressent as 'the chaos of the world'.

Gilt bronze became a favourite medium for the Louis XV clock case, engaging the attention

**Four Continents clock
c. 1720–c. 1725**

of some of the finest sculptors and bronze founders, such as Jacques Caffiéri and Jean-Claude Chambellan, called Duplessis the elder, to the last of whom the cases of the two finest musical clocks in the Collection (pp. 48–51) are attributed. The musical clocks are fairly late examples of the Louis XV style and lack the almost abstract quality of the principal mounts on the huge astronomical clock made for Jean Paris de Monmartel in about 1750 (pp. 44–5); the astronomical clock was somewhat altered at the end of Monmartel's life by the addition of later, more naturalistic mounts and rather tame marquetry.

The transitional period, dating from the end of the 1750s till about 1775, saw a revival of the taste for combining gilt and patinated bronze on the same clock case, a taste more characteristic of the late Louis XIV than of the Louis XV period. The

Astronomical clock c. 1750 (detail)

Employment of Time model (pp. 54–5), originally modelled for the literary hostess Madame Geoffrin at the extraordinarily early date of 1754, the barometer and clock formerly belonging to the Swiss-born baron de Bezenval (pp. 58–61) and the Night and Day clock (pp. 76–7), designed by Le Carpentier after Michelangelo, but following a borrowing made by André-Charles Boulle, are all excellent examples of this combination. Although given to heaviness and slight eccentricity in the design of gilt-bronze mounts, as on the long-case clock with mounts by Philippe Caffiéri (pp. 56–7), some of which have an almost Art Deco appearance, the transitional period in French furniture was a distinguished one, producing on occasion a classic design like the Employment of Time model, which continued to be made for almost thirty years after its introduction in 1754.

Although belonging to the transitional period, both the Avignon clock (pp. 68–9) and the clock with Minerva giving counsel to the youthful Louis XVI (pp. 70–1) seem, by the delicacy of their modelling and the gracefulness of their figures, to anticipate the mature Louis XVI style, even though their elaborate compositions and iconography give them something of the character of public monuments. The Avignon clock was chased and gilded by Pierre Gouthière, the principal creator of the Louis XVI style in gilt bronze. The sums paid to the different artists and craftsmen who worked on the Avignon clock show the costliness of clock cases as opposed to movements. Gouthière was paid 9,200 *livres*, or twenty-five times as much as the clockmaker de Lunésy, who only received 360 *livres*. But Gouthière was also paid over six times as much as Boizot, who made the original sculptural model. This suggests that the execution of a Louis XVI furnishing bronze was more highly valued than the original artist's idea, an exact

The Avignon clock c. 1771

Clock with Minerva and Louis XVI c. 1774

bronze Cupid (pp. 88–9) a casual beholder might be forgiven for not recognising that he was looking at a clock at all. Long-case clocks of the same period show a contrasting tendency, that of revealing as much as possible of the movements by means of glass panels at the fronts and sides of the cases (see pp. 56–7 and 84–5), although the same cases are vehicles for elaborate gilt-bronze mounts as well. The sculptural, allegorising tendency persists in fact, in French eighteenth-century clock cases, with some of the allegories remaining the same throughout the century. The gilt, patinated and enamelled bronze clock of c. 1780 (pp. 82–3), probably cast by Martincourt after a design by Pajou, has Father Time tied up with flower garlands by two winged infants who have seized his hour glass and his scythe, a reworking, in effect, of the Love Triumphing over Time model first introduced by Boulle in about 1695.

reversal of the normal twentieth-century attitude.

The sculptural interpretation of clock cases by no means diminished under Louis XVI, with distinguished sculptors like Étienne-Maurice Falconet and Augustin Pajou apparently supplying original models for clocks. Gilt bronze was now often combined with marble, either real or simulated (see pp. 64–5, 68–71, 76–83, 86–9 and 96–7), or with other stones (see pp. 78–81), with enamelling or enamels (see pp. 70–1, 82–3 and 92–3) and with Sèvres or Paris porcelain, either in the form of plaques (see pp. 94–5) or in the form of vases or columns (see pp. 90–1 and 96–7), into which the clock movements were actually inserted. The sculptural character of the cases often led to the abandonment of the traditional clock face in favour of rotating dials which could be combined with a vase, a globe, a cylinder or even a miniature table (see pp. 62–3, 70–1, 74–5, 82–3 and 88–9). This arrangement, which is technically inefficient since the drive is less direct than with an arbor driving hands round a conventional dial, seems almost to deny or conceal the essential character of a timepiece. In the case of the clock and candelabrum with the large

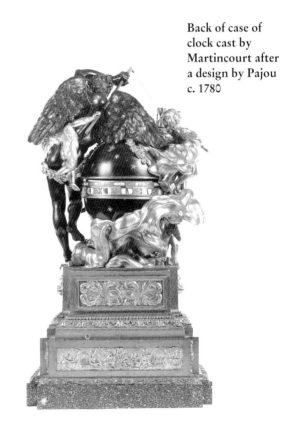

Back of case of clock cast by Martincourt after a design by Pajou c. 1780

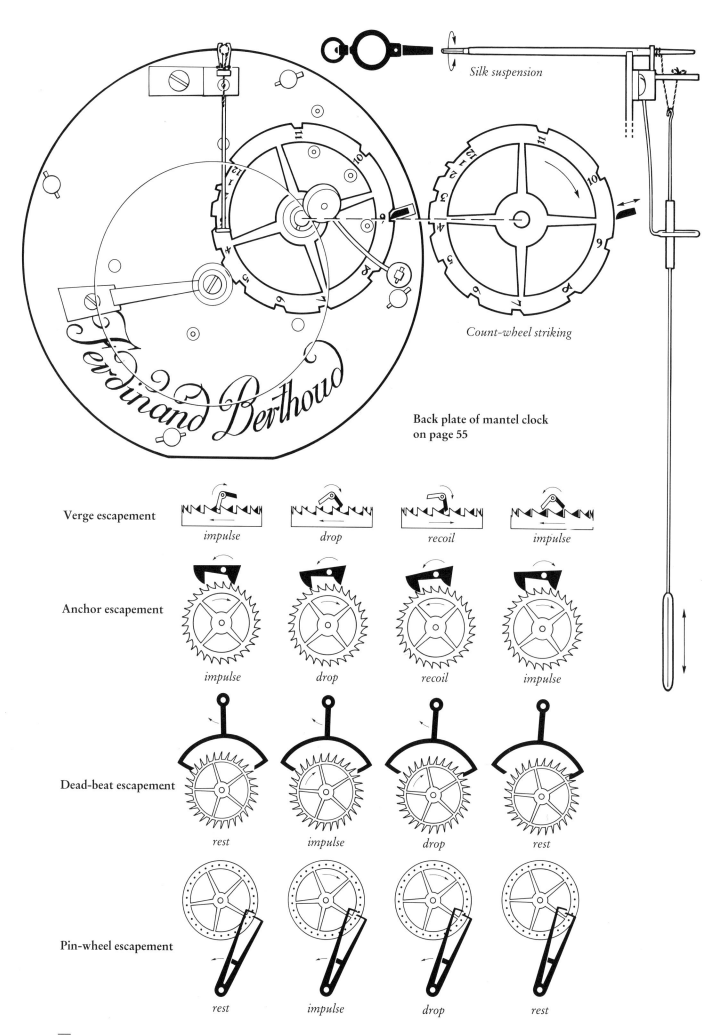

Silk suspension

Count-wheel striking

Back plate of mantel clock
on page 55

Verge escapement

impulse   *drop*   *recoil*   *impulse*

Anchor escapement

impulse   *drop*   *recoil*   *impulse*

Dead-beat escapement

rest   *impulse*   *drop*   *rest*

Pin-wheel escapement

rest   *impulse*   *drop*   *rest*

Clock Movements and Barometers in Eighteenth-century France

Like other European clockmakers, French eighteenth-century *horlogers* were the beneficiaries of a Dutch invention of the mid-seventeenth century, the application of the pendulum to clock movements by the astronomer and mathematician Christian Huygens, which transformed the accuracy of both weight-driven and spring-driven clocks. In 1657 Salomon Coster made the first weight-driven pendulum clock for Huygens, who in the following year published his treatise *Horologium*, incorporating a detailed design for a pendulum clock. With Coster's spring-driven pendulum clocks, the improvement in accuracy was even more marked, spring-driven clocks having previously been inaccurate, owing to the greater force exerted by a spring when fully wound than when nearly unwound. The pendulum was quickly adopted by French clockmakers and greatly stimulated the production of clocks, which had previously been called *horloges*, but now began to be called *pendules* in tribute to the new invention. The new pendulum clocks had large dials which could be read across a room, fitted, unlike most earlier clocks, with minute hands, introducing an entirely new attitude to timekeeping. Louis XIV does not appear to have been interested in clocks, although he granted Huygens a pension, nor to have understood their significance for the advancement of science, but his obsessive punctuality, described by Saint-Simon, was made possible by the new accuracy of his timepieces.

The earliest pendulum clocks made use of the verge

Back plate of movement from Filing-cabinet clock c. 1766–7 (pp. 52–3)

escapement, invented in the late thirteenth century, which first made mechanical clockwork possible, but in about 1670 one of the London clockmakers invented the anchor escapement, in which the pallets at either end of a steel anchor engage alternately with the teeth on the escape wheel. This invention was also adopted by French clockmakers, reducing the arc which the pendulum had to perform and achieving greater accuracy. Quite often French clockmakers continued to use the verge escapement (see pp. 26–7 and 38–9), possibly because it did not, unlike the anchor, require the clock to be exactly level. Although French clockmakers of the late seventeenth and early eighteenth centuries did not match the technical achievements of the greatest London clockmakers such as Thomas Tompion and George Graham, their movements are well made and accurate as timekeepers. The standard eighteenth-century French clock movement, well represented in the Wallace Collection, is spring-driven, with an anchor escapement and a silk pendulum suspension, enabling the pendulum to be lengthened or shortened by turning the arbor, from which it is suspended by a loop of thread, through an adjustment hole at the top of the dial. The same movement generally has a spring-driven striking train, controlled by a count wheel, a device invented in the fourteenth century to enable a striking train to strike the number of strokes corresponding to the actual number of the hour. Some of the movements in the Collection also strike the quarters, requiring a second striking train and count wheel for that purpose. Where a movement in the Wallace Collection departs from this standard type, it is often as the result of nineteenth-century alterations. Twenty-three of the spring-driven movements have had their silk suspensions replaced by steel-spring suspensions, with the pendulum hanging from a flexible strip of steel. The other common alteration is the fitting of a dead-beat escapement in place of an original anchor escapement. This type of escapement, invented by the London clockmakers Thomas Tompion and Richard Townley in the early 1670s and perfected by George Graham in 1715, resembles an anchor escapement, but has the pallets designed in such a way that, with each swing of the pendulum, they no longer push the escape wheel back in the wrong direction, causing a recoil. It was not widely adopted by the French in the eighteenth century, but was fitted to nine of the Wallace Collection clock movements in the nineteenth century (see pp. 28–31, 34–5, 42–5, 48–9, 60–1, 72–3 and 88–9).

The making of clocks was more specialised in eighteenth-century Paris than is commonly realised. The steel springs, expensive items in an age before the mass production of high-grade steel, were made by specialist makers, whose scratched signatures are sometimes found on them (see pp. 42–3, 48–51, 54–5 and 78–9). The quality of these springs was high, so that, even when ready for rewinding, they did not cause the movements to lose time seriously. This enabled French clockmakers to

Detail of compensating pendulum from Long-case clock and barometer c. 1768 (pp. 56–7)

dispense with the fusee, a cone-shaped equalising device, which transmits the power from the fully-wound spring through minimum leverage and the power from the unwound spring through maximum leverage. The absence of this device from French eighteenth-century clock movements is one of the most immediately noticeable differences from English movements of the same period. The fusee is, however, used in the carillons of the two French musical clocks in the Collection, to ensure that the different tunes in their repertoire are played at a constant speed. The dials and their enamel numbers were bought in by the clockmakers, as already noted, while the elegant signatures on the backplates of the movements were carried out by specialist engravers. Certain clockmakers specialised in certain types of movement, so that the carillons of the two musical clocks were made by different makers from those who produced their going and striking trains. With the astronomical clock, Stollewerck, who specialised in astronomical movements and in carillons, drew on the assistance of Alexandre Fortier, a Parisian notary and inventor. Strictly speaking the clock is a planisphere, since its principal dial projects the Northern hemisphere onto a plane, rather than showing the orbits of the planets round the sun. The clock also gives the equation of time, the difference between mean time and true solar time, which can run up to sixteen minutes ahead of mean time and up to fourteen minutes behind, depending on the season. The striking train strikes the hours in solar time, implying that the latter was still the time by which Frenchmen then regulated their lives.

In the second half of the eighteenth century French clockmakers endeavoured to rival the technical achievements of English ones. The most important area of rivalry, only marginally relevant to the clocks in the Wallace Collection, but directly affecting the colonial struggle between the two nations, was the development of the marine chronometer, which, by working accurately on board a sailing ship, would enable the crew to calculate, by comparison with the sun at midday, the number of degrees of longitude they had travelled. The English clockmaker, John Harrison, was ahead of the French in the making of chronometers, but Pierre Le Roy carried out extensive research into the principles involved. Le Roy's rival in this field in France was the Swiss-born Ferdinand Berthoud, an able clockmaker, but with less real understanding of marine chronometry. In 1770 Berthoud was appointed *Horloger Mécanicien du Roy et de la Marine*, an appointment he appears to have anticipated by having the dials of his other clocks decorated with gold *fleurs-de-lis* (see pp. 56–7 and 64–5). The long-case clock with a movement by Berthoud (pp. 56–7) incorporates a number of refinements, including a type of pendulum invented by John Harrison which uses the different expansion rates of steel and brass to compensate for changes in temperature. Such weight-driven, long-case clocks were the most accurate clocks of the eighteenth century, as their name *régulateurs* implies; they were used for regulating other timepieces. Both the Berthoud clock and the long-case clock with movement by Lepaute de Bellefontaine (pp. 84–5) originally had centre seconds hands, indicating even greater confidence in their accuracy, although the seconds hand on the Berthoud clock is now missing. The same clock has a Graham-type dead-beat escapement, while the movement by Lepaute de Bellefontaine has a recoilless pin-wheel escapement, in which a series of pins on the face of the escape wheel have to pass between pallets forming a gate, swinging from side to side. This escapement, a type of dead-beat, was favoured by a number of French clock-makers in the late eighteenth century and is found on a movement by another member of the Lepaute family (pp. 86–7), as well as on a much earlier movement by Jean Jolly (pp. 20–1), where it is probably a later alteration.

The long-case clock with movement by Berthoud

Detail of thermometer from Mantel Barometer and Thermometer c. 1780 (pp. 80–1)

incorporates a barometer at the left of the pendulum case. The mercuric barometer, which measures variations in atmospheric pressure by means of mercury in a glass tube open at one end, had been invented by Evangelista Torricelli, a pupil of Galileo, in 1643. The rise and fall of the mercury in the glass tube is translated into rotary movement on a dial by means of a float on the surface of the mercury in the short, open section of the tube. The float has a cord attached to it which passes over a small pulley, with a weight at the other end of the cord to keep it taught. A needle pointing to the weather condition on the dial is attached to the pulley, so that the rise or fall of the mercury registers on the dial. The barometer greatly appealed to the scientific spirit of the second half of the seventeenth century and was taken up as an ornament for interiors in about 1680. The barometer column had to be high enough to take a glass tube enclosing a column of mercury 30 inches high. The front of the column was thus suitable for mounting a thermometer, to allow comparisons between the two instruments (see pp. 16–17, 46–7, 66–7 and 80–1). Because both barometers and thermometers required some sort of dial or scale, which could conveniently be made in enamelled metal, both instruments became the prerogative of the guild of enamellers, although the makers of such instruments came to regard themselves as being rather above ordinary enamellers. The craftsmen employed on making the cases for barometers depended, as with clock cases, on the materials used. In the eighteenth century, clocks and barometers began to be made in matching pairs (see pp. 58-61 and 78–81), and eventually to be combined in the same case (pp. 56–7), a logical combination, since both instruments assert Man's recently acquired power over his environment, a power founded on accurate measurement.

BAROMETER AND THERMOMETER *(BAROMÈTRE ET THERMOMÈTRE)*

c. 1710

H. 114 cm.(44⅞ in.) W. 53.5 cm.(21⅛ in.) D. 42 cm. (16½ in.)

Pearwood case veneered at the front with Boulle marquetry of brass and tortoiseshell and at the back with oak, with gilt-bronze mounts.
Barometer dial signed by Bianchi (recorded 1850–60); case attributed to André-Charles Boulle (1642–1732). The left-hand female figure stamped PIRET, *recording repairs by Jules Piret (recorded 1856–70).*

Although the barometer dial and its accompanying enamel plaques were replaced by Bianchi in the mid-nineteenth century, the case is almost certainly by André-Charles Boulle. It is mounted above the dial with a gilt-bronze satyr's mask of a model also found on the sides of the so-called *pendule de Robert de Cotte*, a clock attributable to Boulle that corresponds in design to a drawing for a clock, probably by Pierre Lepautre, in the Robert de Cotte collection in the Bibliothèque Nationale. Although the original owner of the barometer remains unknown, there are three *fleurs-de-lis* in the marquetry at the bottom and a single *fleur-de-lis* on the blued steel band retaining the bulb of the thermometer tube. The female figures seated on the edges of the case above the dial represent Astronomy and Geometry, although the instruments they hold are merely lacquered, not gilded, and were probably added in the nineteenth century. The thermometer on the front of the shaft is, however, quite unaltered and is engraved with a temperature scale which is probably that of the *échelle de*

Detail of dial

Florence, widely used before the invention of the Réaumur scale in 1731. The scale on this thermometer goes up to twenty-five degrees, which on the Réaumur scale would only be equivalent to about nineteen degrees centigrade.

The barometer was in the Parisian collection of the 4th Marquess of Hertford by 1865, when he lent it to the Musée Rétrospectif, an exhibition of decorative art of the past held at the Palais de l'Industrie.

F15

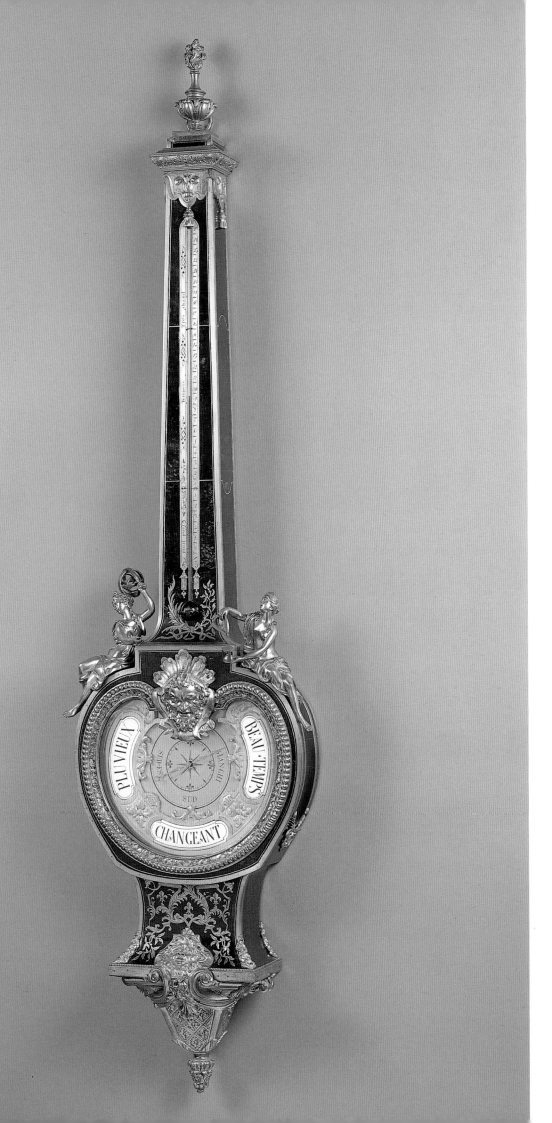

CLOCK AND PEDESTAL (*PENDULE ET SA GAÎNE*)

c. 1712–c. 1720

Clock: H. 100.2 cm.(39½ in.) W. 52 cm.(20½ in.) D. 31 cm.(12¹³⁄₆₄ in.)
Pedestal: H. 133 cm.(52⅜ in.) W. 65.5 cm.(25⅝ in.) D. 43.5 cm.(17⅛ in.)

Oak veneered with Boulle marquetry of brass and tortoiseshell, with gilt-bronze mounts.
Movement signed THURET, *probably for Jacques-Augustin Thuret* (horloger du roi *1694, d. 1739);*
clock case and pedestal attributed to André-Charles Boulle (1642–1732).

The clock case here is an example of the richer version of Boulle's Love Triumphing over Time model made between 1712 and 1720. The model, showing Love flying away with Time's scythe and Time left holding the scales, was originally made in the 1690s for Nicolas Desmarets, a nephew of Colbert; the richer version differs from the original one in having gilt-bronze acanthus sprays framing the front of the clock case, a gilt-bronze drapery with scalloped edge below Time, clenched fingers on Time's left hand and a twisted suspension cord on his scales. The original model is represented in the Wallace Collection by the mantel clock (pp. 30–1), which has, rather confusingly, a movement dated 1726. It seems that the master models for the richer version were probably destroyed in the fire in Boulle's workshop in the Louvre in August 1720 and that Boulle reverted thereafter to making the original version. On both versions in the Wallace Collection, Love has unfortunately lost Time's scythe.

The handsome pedestal certainly belongs with the clock, since the Louvre possesses a long-case clock, made for the comte de Toulouse, an illegitimate son of Louis XIV, which combines the shapes of Wallace Collection clock and pedestal in a single clock case. The marquetry on the sides of the pedestal, showing

Clock shown on its pedestal

the winged cap of Mercury above a trophy of musical instruments, also appears on the pedestal of a clock by André-Charles Boulle in the Musée National des Techniques, the design of which has been attributed to Gilles-Marie Oppenordt (1672–1742).

The clock movement has a twenty-eight-day, spring-driven going train and a count wheel striking train, striking the hours and half-hours on a bell mounted above the back plate. The movement has an anchor escapement and a steel-spring pendulum suspension, although the adjustment hole for the original silk suspension can be seen in the enamel plaque for XII on the dial.

The clock and pedestal are probably those listed on the landing of the grand staircase of Dorchester House after the death of the 3rd Marquess of Hertford in 1842 and would have passed to the 4th Marquess by descent.

F43 and F55

Mantel Clock (*pendule de cheminée*)

c. 1715

H. 79 cm.(31⅛ in.) W. 53.5 cm.(21⅛ in.) D. 42 cm.(16½ in.)

Oak case veneered with rosewood, tortoiseshell, ebony and brass, with gilt-bronze mounts.
Movement signed by Jean Jolly (maître 1698); case attributed to André-Charles Boulle (1642–1732).

This model of clock corresponds to an entry for an unfinished '*boëte de pandulle historiée d'une Vénus avec son amour*' in the inventory attached to Boulle's 1715 Act of Renunciation, by which he made over his property to his four sons. The master models for the Venus and Cupid are then listed in Boulle's probate inventory of 1732, having evidently survived a major fire in his workshop in August 1720. The strongly sculptural character of the case, with the figures dominating the clock dial, anticipates many later French clock designs; two other surviving examples of this clock show that the Venus and Cupid would originally have been more more closely linked to the case by a garland of gilt-bronze flowers running down from the chaplet held by Venus to join the flowers on the left of the case, as well as by another running down from the chaplet and passing behind Cupid's right arm. The beautiful dial, cast with six flying infants in low relief each support-ing an even hour number, is also strongly sculptural, but is in fact of a model sometimes found on examples of Boulle's original

Back plate of movement

version of the Love Triumphing over Time clock.

The clock movement has an eight-day, spring-driven going train and a count-wheel striking train, striking the hours and half-hours on a single bell. The movement has a pin-wheel escapement, probably fitted in the late eighteenth century, and a steel-spring pendulum suspension, replacing a silk suspension which would have been adjusted by the regulating hand just below XII on the dial.

The clock belonged in the mid-nineteenth century to Prince Anatole Demidoff at the Palazzo San Donato, Florence, and was bought by Mannheim for the 4th Marquess of Hertford at the San Donato sale in Paris in March 1870.

F93

Venus Marina
French bronze c. 1710
The J. Paul Getty Museum

CLOCK WITH THE THREE FATES (*PENDULE À PARQUES*)

c. 1715

Clock: H. 49 cm.(19¼ in.) W. 59 cm.(23¼ in.) D. 33.5 cm.(13¼ in.)

Oak case veneered with ebony and with brass stringings, with gilt-bronze mounts. Movement signed by Jean Moisy (1714–82, maître 1753); case attributed to André-Charles Boulle (1642–1732).

This model of clock, with its figures of the Fates or Parcae spinning the thread of human life and then cutting it, has been identified with the '*pendule à Parques du modèle de M. Coustou*', listed in Boulle's Act of Renunciation of 1715 and in his probate inventory of 1732. The high quality of the figures of the Fates, Clotho with her distaff at the left, Lachesis with a bobbin at the top and Atropos with her shears at the right, would thus be explained by the original models having been supplied either by the sculptor Nicolas Coustou (1658–1733) or by his younger brother, Guillaume (1677–1746). Unfortunately the Fates have lost the gilt-bronze thread which originally linked them and was the reason for their gestures. Given the early date of the case, the movement by Moisy cannot be the original one, but was probably fitted c. 1766, a date which is scratched on the going spring. In 1775 the clock was in the collection of Randon de Boisset and was supported on a *bas d'armoire* or low cabinet. The clock was in London between 1834 and 1845 and was fitted with a new dial, signed on the back by J. Merfield of 5 Radcliffe Terrace, Goswell Road, but painted on the front with a fake mark, *LE ROY A PARIS*; probably at the same time the clock was placed on top of a filing cabinet by André-Charles Boulle, itself altered by the addition of a drop-front and of

**André-Charles Boulle (1642–1732)
Bracket clock, with the Three Fates as on the drop front of F413**
Musée du Louvre, Paris

shallow, internal drawers. On the drop-front a London cabinetmaker fixed a low-relief mount of the three Fates, probably removed from the front of a Boulle clock of a completely different model. The whole piece of furniture was then moved to Paris, probably by the 12th Earl of Pembroke.

The clock movement has an eight-day, spring-driven going train, with an anchor escapement and a steel-spring pendulum suspension. The movement is now wound below the dial to the right, the winding being transferred through two gears to the original winding train at the back. A calendar ring appears to have been formerly driven off the going train, but has itself been removed.

The clock and filing cabinet were bought for the 4th Marquess of Hertford at the Parisian sale of the 12th Earl of Pembroke in June–July 1862.

F413

Back plate of movement

WARDROBE CLOCK (*RÉGULATEUR EN ARMOIRE*)

c. 1715

H. 311.5 cm.(112 ½in.) W. 196 cm.(77 ½in.) D. 65.8 cm.(25 ⅞in.)

Oak wardrobe, veneered with ebony and contre-partie *Boulle marquetry of tortoiseshell and brass, mounted with gilt-bronze mounts and fitted in the centre with a clock. Movement signed by Pierre Gaudron (maître 1695, d.1745); wardrobe attributed to André-Charles Boulle (1642–1732).*

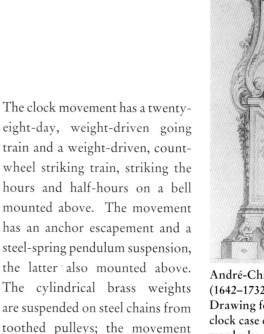

André-Charles Boulle (1642–1732) Drawing for the clock case of a wardrobe clock
Musée des Arts Décoratifs, Paris

The wardrobe is the second item in the inventory accompanying Boulle's Act of Renunciation of 1715, the first being a *première-partie* marquetry wardrobe which originally accompanied it. The first wardrobe was valued at 5,000 *livres*, the present one at 4,000, a difference which reflected the cost of tortoiseshell, which is used more lavishly in *première-partie* marquetry, where it forms the background, than in *contre-partie*. The two wardrobes were probably made for Moyse-Augustin de Fontanieu (1662–1725) and Jean Delpech (?1671–1737), both named in Boulle's probate inventory of 1732 in connection with bronze master models for wardrobe mounts weighing 129 pounds. The key of the Wallace Collection wardrobe is cast with lions on its bow, suggesting that it may be for Jean Delpech, a councillor in the Paris *Parlement*, whose arms had lions as supporters. A drawing attributed to Boulle in the Musée des Arts

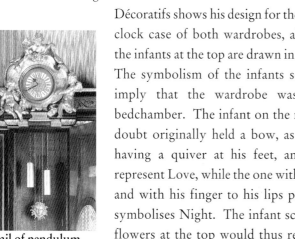

Décoratifs shows his design for the central clock case of both wardrobes, although the infants at the top are drawn in reverse. The symbolism of the infants seems to imply that the wardrobe was for a bedchamber. The infant on the right no doubt originally held a bow, as well as having a quiver at his feet, and must represent Love, while the one with an owl and with his finger to his lips probably symbolises Night. The infant scattering flowers at the top would thus represent Dawn, by analogy with Aurora.

Detail of pendulum and weights

The clock movement has a twenty-eight-day, weight-driven going train and a weight-driven, count-wheel striking train, striking the hours and half-hours on a bell mounted above. The movement has an anchor escapement and a steel-spring pendulum suspension, the latter also mounted above. The cylindrical brass weights are suspended on steel chains from toothed pulleys; the movement is wound by pulling the chains manually. The dial is a nineteenth-century replacement, the enamel numerals being painted in a rather light blue colour.

The wardrobe clock was re-united with its *première-partie* companion in the sale of the dealer Vincent Donjeux in April 1793, but they were separated again in the nineteenth century. The wardrobe clock was inventoried in Hertford House after the death of the 4th Marquess of Hertford in 1870.

F429

PEDESTAL CLOCK (PENDULE)

c. 1715–c. 1720

H. 86 cm.(33⅞in.) W. 56 cm.(22in.) D. 20 cm.(7⅞in.)

Oak case veneered with Boulle marquetry of brass and tortoiseshell, with gilt-bronze mounts and glass panels at the front and sides.
Movement signed Vidal A Paris, *perhaps for the father of Jacques-Augustin Vidal* (fils de maître *1776); case by an unidentified cabinetmaker.*

The clock has been subjected to a number of alterations and was probably associated with its present pedestal in the mid-nineteenth century. It may, however, have been the clock bequeathed to a Monsieur Graillet by the clockmaker Antoine II Gaudron in his will dated 31 March 1748. The clock in the will is described as having three figures, namely a celestial Virtue, possibly the winged Fame on top of the present clock, a figure of Justice, seen on the right of the clock, and one of Prudence, seen on the left. Although the figures have lost some of their attributes, Justice is identifiable by the scales in her left hand and Prudence by the serpent in her left. The clock in the bequest also had a relief of Time carrying off Truth, though it is unclear whether the relief was on the pedestal which then supported the clock or on the clock itself. Possibly it was on the front of the clock where there is now a later bearded mask attached with large screws. The clock in the bequest had a movement striking the quarters, as well as the hours and half-hours, but the movement of the present clock has been replaced twice. In the 1890 and 1898 Hertford House inventories it is described as having a chiming movement with eight bells.

The clock movement has an eight-day, spring-driven going train and a count-wheel striking train, striking

Back plate of movement

the hours and half-hours on a bell mounted above. The movement has a verge escapement and a silk pendulum suspension, which cannot, however, be adjusted through the regulation hole in the enamel plaque for XII on the dial.

The clock and its present pedestal were inventoried in Hertford House after the death of the 4th Marquess of Hertford in 1870.

F44

Pedestal Clock (*pendule et sa gaîne*)

c. 1720–c. 1725

Clock: H. 125 cm.(49¼ in.) W. 66 cm.(26in.) D. 30.5 cm.(12¼ in.)
Pedestal: H. 165.5 cm.(65 in.) W. 70.2 cm.(27⅝ in.) D. 33 cm.(13 in.)

Oak veneered with tortoiseshell and Boulle marquetry of brass and tortoiseshell,
with gilt-bronze mounts.
Movement signed by Louis Mynuel (c. 1675–1742, marchand horloger
privilégié du Roi suivant la Cour 1705); case and pedestal attributed to
André-Charles Boulle (1642–1732).

The clock is mounted with the Four Continents, Europe with fur-lined cap and holding a sceptre, Asia with plumed turban and holding a scimitar, Africa crowned with an elephant's head and America with a feathered headdress and skirt. The clock is one of a group of five of this model, the best-known, originally with a movement by Julien Le Roy, being in the Bibliothèque de l'Arsenal, Paris. The Arsenal clock and two others have oval dials, with self-lengthening hour hands mounted in separate sleeves. One other clock, at Waddesdon Manor, resembles the present one in having a round dial and the Waddesdon and Wallace Collection clocks are the only two to have gilt-bronze bows, oval medallions with an alligator and a rearing horse and pendants of flowers over their glazed sides.

The rearing horse is a symbol of Europe, the alligator one of America and the theme of the world is continued on the pedestal with a medallion of Hercules relieving Atlas.

The mounts on this group of clocks do not appear on other furniture attributed to Boulle, but the marquetry on the back door of the Wallace Collection clock is of the same design as the *contre-partie* marquetry on the middle of the doors of the wardrobe (pp. 24–5).

The clock movement has an eight-day, spring-driven going train and two count-wheel striking trains, one striking the hours on a bell in the hood, the other the quarters on two bells, also in the hood. The movement has a dead-beat escapement and a steel-spring pendulum suspension with Brocot adjustment, but the adjustment hole for the original silk suspension is just below XII on the dial.

The clock and pedestal were presented in 1770 to the town of Yverdon, Switzerland, by Monsieur Perrinet-de-Faugnes, administrator of the salt works in the Franche-Comté; sold by the town in 1866 to the dealer Barlier, of Lyons, they were bought by the 4th Marquess of Hertford from the Parisian dealer, Miallet, in late 1866 or early 1867.

F42

Marquetry on back panel of clock

Medallion with alligator between Africa and Europe

Mantel Clock (*PENDULE DE CHEMINÉE*)

c. 1726

H. 89.8 cm.(35⅜ in.) W. 56.2 cm.(22⅛ in.) D. 23.7 cm.(9²¹⁄₆₄ in.)

Oak case veneered with ebony and with première-partie *Boulle marquetry of brass and tortoiseshell, with gilt-bronze mounts; supported on a pinewood plinth veneered with ebony and with* contre-partie *Boulle marquetry.*
Movement signed by Claude Martinot (valet de chambre horloger ordinaire du Roi 1725, died 1744) and dated 1726; case attributed to André-Charles Boulle (1642–1732).

This clock is a late example of the original, simpler version of Boulle's Love Triumphing over Time design, a drawing for which exists in the Musée des Arts Décoratifs, and may be compared with the richer version on its pedestal (pp. 18–19). The allegorical concept of these clocks has been shown to derive from a woodcut by Nicolò Vicentino (active 1510–1550), reprinted by Andrea Andreani in 1608 and based on a now obliterated fresco by Pordenone on the façade of the Palazzo d'Anna in Venice. The woodcut shows Love seizing the scales from the grasp of the recumbent Time; the clocks alter the allegory somewhat by having Love flying away with Time's scythe rather than seizing the scales, which, on the clocks, Time has managed to retain. The figure of Time, designed by François Girardon (1628–1715), also resembles the principal figure of his Basin of Saturn at Versailles of 1672–7.

The pinewood plinth is a nineteenth-century addition,

André-Charles Boulle (1642–1732)
Design for a clock representing Love Triumphing over Time
Musée des Arts Décoratifs, Paris

but uses a gilt-bronze egg-and-dart moulding which is probably original.

The clock movement has an eight-day, spring-driven going train and two count-wheel striking trains, one striking the hours on a single bell, the other the quarters on two bells. The movement has a Brocot escapement and a steel-spring pendulum suspension, replacing an original silk suspension.

The clock was inventoried in the apartment at no. 2 rue Laffitte after the death of the 4th Marquess of Hertford.

F41

Back plate of movement

BRACKET CLOCK (*PENDULE EN CARTEL*)

c. 1730

H. 77 cm.(30⅛ in.) W. 42.5 cm.(16¾ in.) D. 20.5 cm.(8¾₄ in.)

Oak case veneered with Boulle marquetry of brass and tortoiseshell,
with gilt-bronze mounts.
Movement signed by Jacques Gouchon (recorded 1723); case attributed
to Charles Cressent (1685–1768).

This clock is of the same model as one at Waddesdon Manor and both clocks bear a pronounced resemblance to one of Cressent's gilt-bronze cartel clock designs, which also has a diaper pattern within its pediment and diaper-patterned panels either side of a female mask below the dial. The Waddesdon clock has retained gilt-bronze winged infants seated on the scallop shells at the front corners and both clocks formerly had similar winged infants on the shells at the back corners; the screw holes for holding the infants can be clearly seen on the Wallace Collection clock. A gilt-bronze sunflower under both clocks suggests that they were bracket clocks intended to be mounted quite high on a wall; the clockmaker's name is probably at the bottom of the dial of the Wallace Collection clock for the same reason.

The clock movement has an eight-day, spring-driven going train and a count-wheel striking train, striking the hours and half-hours on a bell in the upper compartment of the case. The movement has an anchor escapement and a steel-spring pendulum suspension, replacing a silk suspension formerly adjusted by a regulator cog which is still mounted on the back of the dial plate.

Left side of case

Back plate of movement

The clock was bought for the 4th Marquess of Hertford at the Parisian sale of the 12th Earl of Pembroke in June 1862.

F409

MANTEL CLOCK (*PENDULE DE CHEMINÉE*)

c. 1730–40

H. 122 cm.(48in.) W. 65 cm.(25⅝ in.) D. 38 cm.(15in.)

Oak case and plinth veneered with tortoiseshell and Boulle marquetry of brass and tortoiseshell, with gilt-bronze mounts and glass panels at the front and sides.
Movement signed THURET A PARIS, *probably for Jacques-Augustin Thuret (horloger du Roi 1694, died 1739); case attributed to Bernard I Van Risamburgh (c. 1660–1738).*

The mounts of the clock include Diana and her chariot on top and four does on the plinth supporting the case on their backs. The mounts have been associated with an entry in the January 1738 probate inventory of Bernard I Van Risamburgh describing the master models for the '*pendule aux biches*', or clock with does. The back door of the Wallace Collection clock has marquetry of a cock crowing beneath a canopy, a design also found on the pedestal of a clock formerly in the collection of the Marquess of Linlithgow. The same pedestal is mounted with laurel-crowned female heads of the same model as those on the legs of the bureau of the Elector of Bavaria in the Louvre. Bernard I Van Risamburgh may thus have made both this clock and the electoral bureau, although later versions of the clock, dating after 1738, were probably made by Jean-Pierre Latz.

The clock movement has an eight-day, spring-driven going train and a spring-driven, count-wheel striking train, striking the hours and half-hours on a

Marquetry on back door of case

single bell mounted above. The movement has a half-dead-beat escapement and a steel-spring pendulum suspension, replacing a silk suspension, the adjustment hole for which can be seen at the bottom of the enamel plaque for XII.

The clock belonged to the 4th Marquess of Hertford by 1865, when he lent it to the Musée Rétrospectif exhibition.

F40

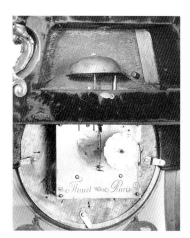

Back plate and bell

Filing Cabinet Clock (PENDULE DE SERRE-PAPIERS)

c. 1740–5

H. 105.7 cm.(41⁵⁄₃₂ in.) W. 94.5 cm.(37¼ in.) D. 30.5 cm.(12¹⁄₆₄ in.)

Oak case veneered with satiné *and purplewood, with gilt-bronze mounts.*
Movement signed by Jean-Baptiste Hervé (1700–80, maître *1726); case attributed*
to Charles Cressent (1685–1768), mounts cast by Jacques Confesseur (c. 1685–1759).

The design of a filing cabinet surmounted by a clock mounted with the figure of Diana as Huntress is fully described in Cressent's own auction sale of March 1757. The description, written by Cressent himself, is worth quoting: 'Firstly, a magnificent writing table and filing cabinet, supporting its own clock, enriched with a figure of Diana holding a bow, with a child about to blow a hunting horn. At the two sides, on an edge of wood, is a stag seized at the throat by a dog. On the other side is a boar, its head seized by a dog, in bronze ...' The same piece was probably offered in Cressent's previous sale of January 1749, but was described in much less detail. The Wallace Collection filing cabinet, which has had doors added at the front over its open pigeonholes and is supported on a bookcase of nineteenth-century manufacture, is not necessarily the example from the 1757 sale, but shows the quality of Cressent's figurative mounts. Cressent, who had trained as a sculptor before becoming a cabinetmaker, would have made the original models for these figures himself, but have subcontracted the casting, chasing and gilding to a bronze founder and a gilder, the founder in this case being Jacques Confesseur.

The clock movement has an eight-day, spring-driven going train and a count-wheel striking train, striking

Back plate of movement

the hours and half-hours on a single bell. The movement has an anchor escapement and a steel-spring pendulum suspension with Brocot adjustment; the original silk suspension would have been adjusted through a hole at the bottom of the enamel plaque for XII on the dial.

The filing cabinet was bought for the 4th Marquess of Hertford at the Cockerell sale at Christie's in May 1848.

F72

CARTEL CLOCK (*CARTEL*)

c. 1740s

H. 110.5 cm.(43½ in.) W. 50.3 cm.(19¾ in.) D. 22 cm.(8²¹⁄₃₂ in.)

Gilt-bronze case, with an oak frame behind.
Movement signed FIEFFE DE L'OBSERVATOIRE *for Jean-Jacques Fiéffé*
(*maître 1725, d. 1770*).

The clock case is probably contemporary with the cartel clocks of Charles Cressent, but does not match their quality as sculpture, particularly in its figures of a huntsman and his hound pursuing a winged dragon. The clockmaker, Fiéffé, supplied clocks to the Paris Observatory in 1732 and 1738, which is probably why he added '*De l'Observatoire*' to his signature on this movement. A number of redundant holes at the top left of the movement suggest that it may formerly have had a quarter-striking train with repeat mechanism and thus have been intended for the alcove of a bedroom, where the repeat would have been used to tell the time in the dark. The irregular triangular section at the bottom of the case projects inwards towards the wall, so that the gilt-bronze case is not flat at the back. It probably fitted onto a shaped cartouche on the panelling of a bedroom alcove. The present oak frame at the back, with its gilded sides, was perhaps fitted to the case when it was removed from its original location.

Back plate of movement

The clock movement has an eight-day, spring-driven going train and a count-wheel striking train, striking the hours on a single bell mounted above. The movement has a verge escapement, with replacement verge, and a silk pendulum suspension. It may formerly have had a quarter-striking train (see above).

The clock can probably be identified with one listed in store at no. 5 rue Taitbout in August 1871, a year after the death of the 4th Marquess of Hertford.

F91

MANTEL CLOCK (*PENDULE DE CHEMINÉE*)

c. 1745–c. 1750

H. 49.5 cm.(19½ in.) W. 32 cm.(12¹⁹/₃₂ in.) D. 13.5 cm.(5⁵/₁₆ in.)

Gilt-bronze case, with pierced panels lined with pink silk.
Movement signed FURET L'AINE A PARIS, *probably for Jacques Furet* (maître *1710*).

The clock case is mounted on top with three Italian Comedy figures, on the left Harlequin, wearing hat, mask and diaper-patterned costume and holding up a tambourine in his left hand; in the middle Mezzetin, wearing wide, loose cap, ruff, belted tunic over breeches and cloak; and on the right Gilles, with broad-brimmed hat, ruff and long-sleeved tunic over trousers. Two further figures are mounted on the legs. Lélio is on the left, wearing three-cornered hat, coat and wide breeches, and holding a mask in his left hand. He is pointing at Punch, on the right, who is wearing a tall hat, ruff, tasselled tunic and trousers, and is playing a guitar.

The clock movement has an eight-day, spring-driven going train and a spring-driven, count-wheel striking train, striking the hours and half-hours on a single bell mounted above. The movement has an anchor escapement and a steel-spring pendulum suspension, replacing a silk suspension formerly adjusted through a hole above XII on the dial.

The clock was bought for the 4th Marquess of Hertford at the Dowager Countess of Ashburnham sale at Christie's in May 1863.

F90

Back plate of movement

CARTEL CLOCK (*CARTEL*)

c. 1747

H. 135.9 cm.(53²³⁄₆₄ in.) W. 52.7 cm.(20¾ in.) D. 35.6 cm.(14 in.)

Gilt-bronze case, mounted on a frame of oak and pinewood,
the sides veneered with Boulle marquetry of brass and tortoiseshell.
Movement signed Guiot A Paris; *case attributed to*
Charles Cressent (1685–1768).

An example of this model of clock in Cressent's auction sale of January 1749 was catalogued by Cressent himself as 'a magnificent bronze clock, composed in the finest taste; on top is a Cupid seated on clouds and leaning his elbow on an hour glass. Below the dial is the figure of Time, holding his scythe and placed on the chaos of the world, while the feet are formed by two large trees'. The allegory must be influenced by Boulle's Love Triumphing over Time design, two versions of which are illustrated in this book, but the theme is interpreted in terms of the Louis XV style and the whole case conceived as a piece of sculpture. Cressent, who trained as a sculptor before becoming a cabinetmaker, would have modelled the figures himself, but have subcontracted the casting, chasing and gilding to a founder and a gilder. It is curious for a gilt-bronze clock case to be screwed at the back to a wooden frame, veneered with Boulle marquetry panels, but Cressent had had his workshop raided three times by the guild of bronze founders, who suspected him of making objects entirely of gilt bronze. The wooden frame probably enabled him to claim this clock to be a piece of cabinet-making.

Left side of case

Above, gilt-bronze castings from the case, photographed during cleaning.
Left, back plate of movement

The clock movement has an eight-day, spring-driven going train and a count-wheel striking train, striking the hours and half-hours on a single bell mounted above. The movement has a dead-beat escapement and an adjustable steel-spring pendulum suspension, replacing a silk suspension formerly adjusted through a hole in the middle of XII on the dial. The striking spring is signed and dated *Richard août 1747* for Claude Richard (recorded in the rue de la Huchette 1754–72).

The clock was inventoried at no. 2 rue Laffitte in August 1871, a year after the death of the 4th Marquess of Hertford.

F92

Astronomical Clock (*Pendule Astronomique*)

c. 1750

H. 294.5 cm.(116³⁹⁄₆₄ in.) W. 133.5 cm.(52¼ in.) D. 91 cm.(35⅞ in.)

In three sections, resting on a plinth; the top section of gilt bronze with glass panels and bronze figures, the middle section of oak veneered with purplewood, satiné *and pictorial marquetry, with gilt-bronze mounts and bronze infants, the lower section similar to the middle, but without the marquetry, and the plinth of mahogany and pinewood veneered with purplewood and tulipwood, with gilt-bronze mounts. Movement signed by Alexandre Fortier (d. before 1777) and Michel Stollewerck (maître 1746, d. 1768); mounts possibly by Jacques Caffiéri.*

The clock, made for Jean Paris de Monmartel (1690–1766), banker to the French Court, is shown in an engraving of him seated in his *grand cabinet* at the Hôtel Mazarin on the rue Neuve-des-Petits-Champs. It is an outstanding example of the taste of a French tax farmer and financier and combines a complex astronomical train with a case illustrating the themes of Love Triumphing over Time, at the top, and the Four Continents, medallions of which were attached to gilt-bronze garlands formerly held by the infants at the top of the middle section.

Back of movement and astronomical train

Jean Paris de Monmartel in his *grand cabinet*, with the astronomical clock behind him
Engraving by L.-J. Cathelin after M.-Q. de Latour and C.-N. Cochin *fils*, published 1772

The movement has a two-week, weight-driven going train, incorporating automatic maintaining power, and a spring-driven count-wheel striking train, striking the hours and half-hours on a single bell according to solar time. It has a Brocot escapement and a steel-spring suspension for the one-second pendulum, replacing a former knife-edge suspension. The indication of apparent solar time is achieved by a movable carriage on the motion work, its position governed by a kidney-shaped cam. The astronomical train

incorporates a perpetual calendar mechanism. The uppermost dial indicates mean time with the blued steel minute hand and apparent solar time with the gilt-brass hands. The largest dial has a silvered outer ring engraved with the signs of the Zodiac, close to which a small disc, representing the sun, revolves in an anti-clockwise direction. In the centre of the same dial are two silvered rings, the outer one showing the age of the moon and having a silvered disc revolving round it and obscured or revealed by a blued steel one to represent the phases of the moon, the inner one engraved with the hours in two sequences of 1 to 12 and having a planisphere of the Northern hemisphere revolving against it so as to indicate the time at any degree of longitude. The two lowest dials show the rising and setting of the sun and moon, with the calendar openings in-between.

The clock was bought for the 4th Marquess of Hertford at the Stowe sale in August 1848.

F98

Barometer and Thermometer (BAROMÈTRE ET THERMOMÈTRE)

c. 1750s

H. 105.5 cm.(39⅝ in.) W. 23.3 cm.(9¹¹⁄₆₄ in.) D. 6 cm.(2²³⁄₆₄ in.)

Walnut case veneered with tulipwood, with gilt-bronze mounts; replacement dial signed
J. Merfield / 5 Radcliffe Terrace / Goswell Road / London; J. Webb / Pins^tr.

The barometer is essentially of the same type as the Boulle marquetry one (pp. 16–17), with a tall shaft above the dial mounted with a thermometer as well as concealing the barometer tube behind it. The appearance of the later barometer is, however, completely different, with its shaped Louis XV outline and quartered tulipwood veneer, laid with the grain converging towards the dial. The thermometer must have been altered in Paris in the early nineteenth century, since the plate is graduated in centigrade, only adopted legally in France in 1801; the plate is probably of the beginning of the nineteenth century, since it refers to several celebrated temperatures recorded in the eighteenth. The dial was replaced in London between 1834 and 1845, when Merfield was recorded at the address given; J. Webb, who painted it, copied the indications from a French dial, but mistook the abbreviation Vt (*Vent*) for Vc. The engraved plate near the bottom of the case must refer to an earlier dial, since the present one is not divided into three *pouces* (old French inches), but only into two, from 27 to 29.

The barometer was inventoried in Hertford House after the death of the 4th Marquess of Hertford in 1870.

F69

Detail of engraved plate near bottom of case

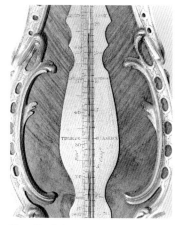

Detail of thermometer

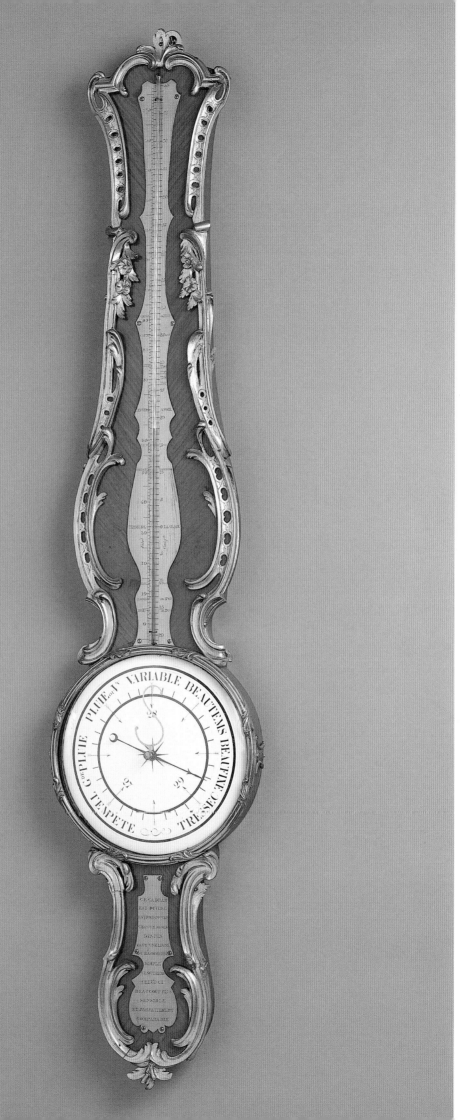

MUSICAL CLOCK (PENDULE À MUSIQUE)

c. 1762

H. 90.5 cm.(35⅝ in.) W. 66 cm.(26in.) D. 30 cm.(11¹³⁄₁₆ in.)

Gilt-bronze case, with pierced panels lined with pink silk.
Movement signed by François Viger (1708–84, maître 1744) with a carillon, which is unsigned;
case possibly designed by Jean-Claude Duplessis père (c. 1690–1774) and cast by François-René Morlay
(maître 1756), whose signature is engraved on the back.

The clock case is close in style to that of the clock in the next entry, the design of which has also been attributed to Duplessis, but whereas that clock is surmounted by two infants, the present one has a spaniel retrieving a game bird on top and the sporting theme is continued with some of the musical instruments at the front corners, notably the horn on the right. The spaniel may be compared with the one flanked by infants on top of the clock of the *bureau du roi* of Louis XV, the mounts of which were modelled by Duplessis. The two Wallace Collection musical clocks are close in date, the clock here having the date 1762 on its going train, the clock in the next entry having 1763 on the back of its dial.

The clock movement has an eight-day, spring-driven going train and a count-wheel striking train, striking the hours and half-hours on a bell mounted above. The movement has a dead-beat escapement and a steel-spring pendulum suspension, replacing a former silk suspension adjusted through a hole in XII on the dial. The going train spring is signed *Richard mars 1762* for Claude Richard (recorded in the rue de la Huchette 1754–72); the spring barrel is similarly dated.

The spring-driven carillon, controlled by a fusee, is set in motion on the hour by a brass rod from the striking train and rotates a brass cylinder, the pins on which operate twenty-five hammers striking on fourteen bells mounted in line just below. The rotation is controlled by a count wheel with a sloping cam on its inner face, which advances the cylinder one position at the end of each tune, so that it can play thirteen different tunes.

Detail of the carillon, with the count wheel at the near end

The clock was in the Parisian collection of the 4th Marquess of Hertford by 1865, when he lent it to the Musée Rétrospectif exhibition.

F97

Back plate of movement, with the brass rod at the left for setting the carillon in motion

MUSICAL CLOCK *(PENDULE À MUSIQUE)*

c. 1763

H. 92 cm.(36¼ in.) W. 69 cm.(27⅛ in.) D. 29.4 cm.(11³⁷/₆₄ in.)

Gilt-bronze case, with pierced panels lined with pink silk.
Movement signed by Pierre Daillé (recorded 1760–5, horloger de Madame la Dauphine),
with dial signed by Joseph Coteau (1740–1812) and dated 1763, and carillon signed by
Michel Stollewerck (maître 1746, d. 1768); case possibly designed by Jean-Claude
Duplessis père (c. 1690–1774).

The case of this clock has long been attributed to Duplessis; this attribution is strengthened by the similarity of the infants on top of it to those crowning the clock on top of the *bureau du roi* of Louis XV, who have similar heads, with the top of the cranium very large in proportion to the face. The present clock has also been compared to a Sèvres porcelain clock in the Louvre supported on hooved legs and probably modelled by Duplessis; the inside edges of the legs of the Sèvres clock are close in shape to the framing of the glass panel at the front of the musical clock.

The movement has an eight-day, spring-driven going train and two spring-driven, count-wheel striking trains, one striking the hours on a single bell on the back plate, the other the quarters on two bells, also on the back plate. The movement has an anchor escapement and a Brocot pendulum suspension, replacing a silk suspension formerly adjusted through a hole below the 60-minute mark. The hour striking spring is signed *Richard 1763* for Claude Richard (recorded in the rue de la Huchette

Signature of Joseph Coteau and date of 1763 on the back of the dial

1754–72). The *Dauphine*, to whom Daillé was appointed clockmaker, was Marie-Josèphe de Saxe (1731–67), married to the son of Louis XV.

The spring-driven carillon, controlled by a fusee, is set in motion on the hour by a copper wire from the hour-striking train and rotates a brass cylinder, the pins on which operate twenty-four hammers striking on fourteen bells mounted in line just below. The rotation is controlled by a count wheel with a sloping cam on its inner face, which advances the cylinder one position at the end of each tune, so that it can play fourteen different tunes.

The clock was bought for the 4th Marquess of Hertford at the Albert sale in Paris in January 1861.

F96

Back of case

Detail of the carillon, with the count wheel at the left end and the spring barrel at the right

Daillé

horloger de Madame
La dauphine

FILING-CABINET CLOCK (*PENDULE DE SERRE-PAPIERS*)

c. 1766–7

H. 182 cm.(71²¹⁄₃₂ in.) W. 91.5 cm.(36 in.) D. 37.5 cm.(14¾ in.)

Clock case of gilt and patinated bronze, supported on an oak filing-cabinet, veneered with tulipwood and mounted with thirty-five soft-paste Sèvres porcelain plaques, twenty-eight with the date letter for 1766, and with two soft-paste Sèvres porcelain trays.
Movement signed Julien Le Roy, *but probably supplied by his son, Pierre Le Roy (1717–85, maître 1737); filing-cabinet by Jean-François Leleu (1729–1807, maître 1764).*

The filing-cabinet has been altered in the nineteenth century by the transfer of sixteen of the porcelain plaques from the sides to the front of the lower stage and by the addition of the doors with the re-decorated porcelain trays to the upper stage. These changes have given the cabinet a slightly garish appearance, whereas the original disposition of the porcelain plaques, with the cabinet abutting a writing-table, would have been more subtle. The cabinet has, however, retained beautiful mounts of gilt and patinated bronze, notably the consoles at the sides, the foliate candelabra arms, which turn back on themselves like those on the *bureau du roi* for Louis XV, and the clock case itself, whose culminating volutes and group of infants also resemble those on the *bureau du roi*, modelled by J.-C. Duplessis or by his son. The right-hand infant has fallen asleep, holding a gilt-bronze book, now missing, on his left knee and leaning his right elbow on a globe. The left-hand infant kneels behind the globe, holding a gilt-bronze cock, which is about to crow. The globe is engraved with a diagram apparently illustrating the measurement of latitude at sea from the angle of the sun in the meridian, while to the left of the globe are two gilt-bronze charts and a telescope. It is appropriate that these maritime allusions should appear above a movement supplied by Pierre Le Roy, who had a consum-

Detail of clock case

ing interest in timekeeping at sea and played a pioneering rôle in the development of the marine chronometer in France.

The movement has an eight-day, spring-driven going train and a count-wheel striking train, striking the hours and half-hours on a steel bell on the back plate. The movement has an anchor escapement and a steel-spring pendulum suspension, replacing a silk one formerly adjusted through a hole in the 60-minute mark on the dial.

The filing-cabinet was bought by E. H. Baldock at the Lord Gwydir sale in May 1829 and then altered by him between 1829 and 1837; it was inventoried in Hertford House after the death of the 4th Marquess of Hertford in 1870.

F71

Mantel Clock (*PENDULE DE CHEMINÉE*)

c. 1768

H. 47.5 cm.(18¾ in.) W. 69.7 cm.(27½ in.) D. 27.8 cm.(10¹⁵⁄₁₆ in.)

Gilt-bronze case, flanked by a patinated bronze figure and supported on an ebony-veneered oak plinth with gilt-bronze mounts.
Movement signed by Ferdinand Berthoud (1727–1807, maître 1753); case designed by Laurent Guiard (1723–88) and cast by Edme Roy (maître 1745); plinth made by Joseph Baumhauer (marchand ébéniste privilégié du roi suivant la cour c. 1749, d. 1772).

This model of clock, originally known as *l'Emploi du Temps*, was designed by Guiard in about 1754 for Madame Geoffrin, whose salon on the rue Saint-Honoré was one of the intellectual centres of Paris, frequented by artists on Mondays and writers on Wednesdays, as well as by distinguished foreigners such as Horace Walpole and Stanislas Poniatowski. Guiard's female figure of the Employment of Time may have been inspired by Nattier's portrait of Madame Geoffrin as Study, painted in 1738. As a result of Madame Geoffrin's influence, numerous examples of the clock were made over a period of nearly thirty years. Madame Geoffrin's own clock, the original, does not appear to have survived, but in 1768 she had another example made for Diderot, described by him as a '*pendule à la Geoffrin*', which is preserved in the Musée du Breuil de Saint-Germain at Langres, Diderot's native town. The Wallace Collection clock, which is dated 1768 on its springs, must be close in date to Diderot's, but while the latter has a plain veneered plinth, the Collection's example has panels of heavy gilt-bronze Vitruvian scrolls, a characteristic motive of early French neo-classicism.

The clock movement has an eight-day, spring-driven going train and a spring-driven count-wheel striking

Back plate of movement

train, striking the hours and half hours on a bell on the back plate. The movement has an anchor escapement and a silk pendulum suspension. Both springs are signed *Brizot octobre 1768*.

The clock was bought by the 3rd Marquess of Hertford at the Countess of Holderness sale in February 1802 and passed to the 4th Marquess by descent.

F267

LONG-CASE CLOCK AND BAROMETER (*RÉGULATEUR AVEC BAROMÈTRE*)

c. 1768

H. 235.5 cm.(92¼ in.) W. 56.4 cm.(22¼ in.) D. 34.8 cm.(13¾ in.)

Oak veneered with ebony, with gilt-bronze mounts.
Movement signed by Ferdinand Berthoud (1727–1807, maître 1753); the case
stamped by Balthazar Lieutaud (maître 1749, d. 1780), gilt-bronze mounts attributed
to Philippe Caffiéri (1714–74).

The clock, an outstanding example of early French neo-classicism, has a number of mounts in common with a long-case clock in the Frick Collection, New York, also stamped by Lieutaud and with a movement by Berthoud, which has a plaque below the top engraved '*Les Bronze* (sic) *Par Caffieri L'aîné 1767*'. Philippe Caffiéri, elder son of Jacques Caffiéri, who had been *sculpteur, fondeur et cizeleur du roi* to Louis XV, was known as *Caffiéri l'aîné* to distinguish him from his younger brother, the portrait sculptor Jean-Jacques Caffiéri. Unlike his father, whose work was in a fully-fledged Louis XV style, demonstrated by the two great chandeliers F83 and F84 in the Wallace Collection, Philippe Caffiéri's bronzes are often in a rather heavy, early neo-classical style, typified here by the frames round the glazed panels with their emphatic right angles and by the hanging laurel pendants of the type known as '*à corde de puits*'. The Frick Collection clock differs from the present one in having a case veneered with tulipwood and surmounted by the chariot of Apollo also found on the long-case clock (pp. 84–5); the relationship of the other mounts on the New York clock to those on the present one is, however, self-evident.

The clock movement has an eight-day, weight-driven going train, fitted with a maintaining power device, and a spring-driven, count-wheel striking train,

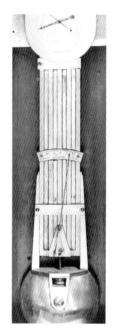

Detail of pendulum

striking the hours and half-hours on a single bell mounted on a bracket above the back plate; the count wheel revolves once every twenty-four hours and thus has twice the normal number of segments. The movement has a dead-beat escapement and a knife-edge pendulum suspension, while the compensating grid-iron pendulum is made up of five steel and four brass rods, the expansion and contraction of which register on a brass temperature gauge on the front. The movement has a calendar dial, turned by a pallet on a shaft driven off the striking-spring barrel, and an equation kidney, attached to the back of the calendar dial and moving a spring-loaded arm which alters the position of the solar-time hand on the dial. The tube for the mercuric barometer is mounted at the front left-hand side of the case and registers on the barometer dial at the top of the middle section.

The clock was inventoried in the apartment at no. 2 rue Laffitte after the death of the 4th Marquess of Hertford.

F271

CARTEL BAROMETER (*BAROMÈTRE EN CARTEL*)

c. 1770

H. 92 cm.(36¼ in.) W. 46 cm.(18⅛ in.) D. 30 cm.(11¹³⁄₁₆ in.)

Case of gilt bronze, with patinated bronze figures.
Barometer dial signed BOURBON A PARIS, *probably for Lange de Bourbon*
(working 1750–70), but the original barometer tube replaced by an English nineteenth-century
aneroid barometer.

The barometer and its accompanying clock are fine examples of French early neo-classical gilt bronze, with expressively modelled bronze infants, but the sculptor, bronze founder and gilder who produced them remain as yet unknown. The infants on the barometer, one of whom is set against a background of gilt-bronze clouds and tips over an urn of water in an obvious reference to the weather, are differentiated from those on the clock by having double insect wings, instead of feathered ones.

The barometer and clock formed part of the estate of the baron de Bezenval (1721–91), who may well have been their original owner, and appear in his posthumous sale in August 1795. Of Swiss origin, the baron served in the Swiss Guards regiment of the French army in the War of the Austrian Succession and in the Seven Years' War; in later life he became a friend of Marie-Antoinette.

The aneroid barometer, fitted to the case in the first half of the nineteenth century, registers changes in atmospheric pressure by means of a vacuum box attached to a spring.

The barometer was bought for the 4th Marquess of Hertford on the thirty-third day of the Stowe sale, 28 September 1848.

F256

CARTEL CLOCK *(CARTEL)*

c. 1770

H. 89.5 cm.(35¼ in.) W. 47.5 cm.(18¾ in.) D. 25.5 cm.(10¾₄ in.)

Case of gilt bronze, with patinated bronze figures.
Movement signed by Michel Stollewerck (maître 1746, d. 1768).

This clock forms a pair with the barometer in the preceding entry and, like the latter, was sold in the baron de Bezenval sale in August 1795. The sale catalogue describes the infant on top of the clock as characterising Fame, which means that he must originally have held a trumpet, the attribute of Fame, in his right hand. The lower infant is gathering together the oak swags framing the clock dial and attaching them below the bezel. It is clear from a clock of the same model in the Louvre that both the present clock and its matching barometer originally had oak-leaf pendants hanging down outside the fluted pilasters at the sides. Indeed on the barometer there is an old fixing-hole for a mount at the inside end of the egg-and-dart moulding above each pilaster.

The clock movement has an eight-day, spring-driven going train and a spring-driven, count-wheel striking train, striking the hours and half-hours on a single bell on the back plate. The movement has a half-dead-beat escapement and a steel-spring pendulum suspension, replacing a silk suspension originally adjusted through a hole above XII on the dial.

Like its matching barometer, the clock was bought for the 4th Marquess of Hertford on the thirty-third day of the Stowe sale, 28 September 1848.

F255

CLOCK WITH ROTATING DIALS *(PENDULE À CADRANS TOURNANTS)*

c. 1770

H. 96 cm.(37¾ in.) W. 34.5 cm.(13¾ in.) D. 34.5 cm.(13¾ in.)

Gilt-bronze case, with rotating dials decorated with paste diamonds; unsigned movement.

Left side of pedestal with infants representing Geography

The clock case, whose designer is unknown, can be dated to about 1770, as it still shows certain features of early French neo-classicism, such as the heavy oak swags partly encircling the medallions on the pedestal. The clock is surmounted by an infant armed as Mars, seated on a pile of military trophies; below the trophies is a cylindrical drum, enclosing the clock movement and mounted at the top with the two rotating dials, the time on which is indicated by a blued steel arrow bolted to the outside of the case. The drum rests in turn on a square classical pedestal, mounted on three sides with relief roundels of infants playing. On the left, two infants, representing Geography, recline beneath a tree, one holding an open book, the other a set square and dividers and

leaning his arm on a terrestrial globe. On the front, two winged infants, representing Astronomy, recline in front of a celestial globe, one holding a protractor, the other a telescope. Finally, on the right, two infants probably representing Love sit by a globe bound with two bands, one with an empty quiver, the other holding a rule.

The clock movement has an eight-day, spring-driven going train and a spring-driven, count-wheel striking train, striking the hours and half-hours on a steel bell on the back plate. The movement has an anchor escapement and a silk pendulum suspension.

The clock was inventoried at no. 2 rue Laffitte in August 1871, a year after the death of the 4th Marquess of Hertford.

F257

MANTEL CLOCK (*PENDULE DE CHEMINÉE*)

c. 1770

H. 69.5 cm.(27⅜ in.) W. 56.8 cm.(22⅜ in.) D. 31.3 cm.(12²¹⁄₆₄ in.)

Gilt-bronze case supported on a bleu turquin *marble base.*
Movement signed by Ferdinand Berthoud (1727–1807, maître 1753, d. 1780).

The clock case supports a reclining figure of Urania, Muse of Astronomy, looking at a scroll engraved with a celestial globe presented to her by a winged infant. This model of clock is perhaps related to one designed by the sculptor Jean-Louis Prieur for the Royal Palace in Warsaw in about 1766. The Warsaw clock, lost in the Second World War, had a figure of Urania, similarly draped and in a similar pose, though in the reverse sense from the figure on the present clock. The clock may thus be tentatively attributed to Prieur and dated a few years later than the Warsaw clock, from which it seems in part to derive. Clocks with figures of Urania were evidently fashionable in the years 1765–70, a model with a standing Urania being among those offered for sale by the clockmaker Jean-André Lepaute in 1766.

The clock movement has an eight-day, spring-driven going train and a spring-driven, count-wheel striking train, striking the hours and half-hours on a steel bell mounted on the back plate. The movement has an anchor escapement and a Brocot pendulum suspension, replacing a silk suspension formerly adjusted through a hole in the middle of the 60-minute mark.

The clock belonged to the 4th Marquess of Hertford by 1867, when he lent it to the Petit Trianon for an exhibition commemorating Marie-Antoinette, arranged under the patronage of the Empress Eugénie.

F266

Back plate of movement

BAROMETER AND THERMOMETER (*BAROMÈTRE ET THERMOMÈTRE*)

c. 1770

H. 102.5 cm.(40 in.) W. 19.8 cm.(7⁵⁄₆₄ in.) D. 5.1 cm.(2¹⁄₆₄ in.)

Pearwood case veneered with marquetry of brass and tortoiseshell, with gilt-bronze mounts; mounted at the front with a spirit thermometer.

The severe design of the barometer case and the angular volutes flanking the top of the shaft suggest that it is an early example of French neo-classicism, dating from c. 1770. This type of barometer, with the dial at the top of the shaft, rather than at the bottom, goes back to the late Louis XIV period. A Louis XIV barometer veneered with brass and tortoiseshell, with the dial at the top above a tapering shaft flanked by gilt-bronze volutes, was in the Charles Stein sale in 1899 and other examples are known. The present barometer also looks back to the Louis XIV period in being veneered with brass and tortoiseshell; the version of Boulle marquetry employed is, however, greatly simplified, consisting largely of alternate bands of the two materials. The dial is also quite traditional in being veneered with Boulle marquetry, with the indications, such as *BEAUTEMS* and *PLUYE*, inserted as individual enamel plaques; the old-fashioned spelling suggests that they are original.

The thermometer is graduated on the Réaumur scale, with the degrees running from minus 15 to 0 and from 0 to 55, with the temperatures engraved in numerals at five-degree intervals up to 50 degrees.

The barometer was inventoried at Hertford House in September 1870, after the death of the 4th Marquess of Hertford.

F380

Detail of dial

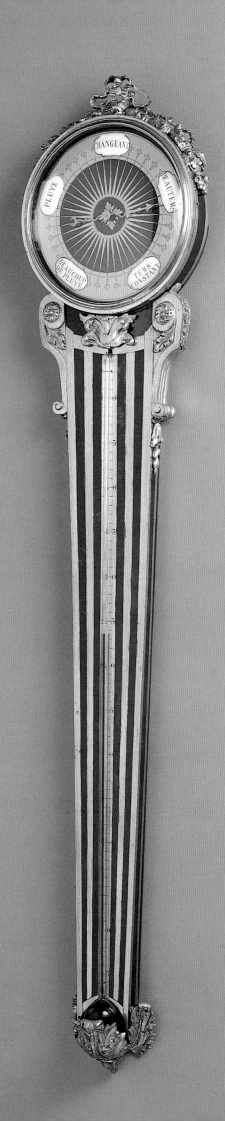

MANTEL CLOCK (*PENDULE DE CHEMINÉE*)

c. 1771

H. 68.5 cm.(27 in.) W. 59 cm.(23¼ in.) D. 33.8 cm.(13¼ in.)

Gilt-bronze case, with a base of Levanto rosso *marble supported on four gilt-bronze feet.*
Movement signed by Nicolas-Pierre Guichon de Lunésy (maître 1764), with enamel dial signed by Joseph Coteau (1740–1812); case designed by Louis-Simon Boizot (1743–1809) and chased and gilded by Pierre Gouthière (1732–c. 1812, maître 1758).

The Avignon clock was made as the result of a dispute between the French Crown and the Holy See, which in 1768 led Louis XV to order the seizure of Avignon and the surrounding Comtat-Venaissin, which had remained Papal possessions since the Middle Ages. The officer taking possession of Avignon was Jean-Louis-Roger, marquis de Rochechouart (1717–76), who then remained governor of the city until April 1774, when it was handed back. During his governorship the marquis so delighted the citizens of Avignon with his urbanity, that on 9 April 1771 the city council agreed that the consular assembly should be entrusted with finding a symbol of the city's gratitude to present to him. On 12 April the consuls decided to present the marquis with a purse containing a hundred gold pieces, but changed their minds the following day in favour of a gilt-bronze clock with ornaments symbolising the city's sentiments towards him. The commissioning of the clock was entrusted to the Avignon-born jeweller Ange Aubert, who in turn commissioned a design by Boizot, which was accepted by the consuls, but with a request for some modifications. A Boizot drawing in the Musée Calvet, Avignon, corresponds closely to the clock and probably represents Boizot's final model. Both the drawing and the clock show a figure symbolising Avignon, recognisable by her mural crown and her

Above, inscription on back of shield held by Avignon.
Left, back of case and back plate of movement

shield with the papal keys, crowning the arms of Rochechouart with an oak-leaf wreath, while below her a river god, the Rhône, and a river goddess, the Durance, symbolise the junction of those two rivers west of Avignon. On the back of Avignon's shield are engraved the names of Boizot and Gouthière, together with the date.

The clock movement has an eight-day, spring-driven going train and a spring-driven, count-wheel striking train, striking the hours and half-hours on a steel bell on the back plate. The movement has an anchor escapement and a Brocot pendulum suspension, replacing a silk suspension formerly adjusted through a hole in the dial plate above the 60-minute mark.

The Avignon clock belonged to the 4th Marquess of Hertford by 1865, when he lent it to the Musée Rétrospectif exhibition.

F258

MANTEL CLOCK *(PENDULE DE CHEMINÉE)*

c. 1774

H. 60.5 cm.(23⅞ in.) W. 51.8 cm.(20⅜ in.) D. 22 cm.(8²¹∕₃₂ in.)

White marble case mounted with gilt and enamelled bronze.
Unsigned movement; design of the case attributed to
Louis-Simon Boizot (1743–1809).

Louis XVI and
Marie-Antoinette at dinner
with the comte and comtesse
de Provence and the comte
and comtesse d'Artois

The clock case shows Minerva giving counsel to the youthful Louis XVI. The king is dressed as a Roman general, but is clearly identified as monarch, since his right hand rests on the tiller of the state, emblazoned on each side with three *fleurs-de-lis*, while to the left the crown, sceptre and hand of justice are supported on a low pillar mounted with gilt-bronze *fleurs-de-lis*. The figures are not unlike those in J.-B. Lemoyne's great painting of 1729, *Louis XV giving peace to Europe*, in the *Salon de la Paix* at Versailles, in which Louis XV is dressed in Roman armour, with one hand on the tiller of the state, while Minerva is similarly posed to the Minerva on this clock. There can be no doubt that the king on the clock is Louis XVI, since the three reliefs on the base refer directly to him. The left-hand relief shows Louis XVI at dinner with Marie-Antoinette, with the king's younger brothers, the comte de Provence and the comte d'Artois, sitting between them, accompanied by their consorts. The relief at the front shows Louis XVI, again in Roman military dress, dictating laws to France from an open book held by Justice, while that at the right shows him gesturing towards six allegorical figures, including Religion, Public Felicity, Hope, Prudence and Liberality, while Cupid, at the left of the relief, inscribes the names of five children in an open book held by Time. The optimistic iconography of the clock leaves no doubt that it dates from the beginning of Louis XVI's reign.

The clock movement has an eight-day, spring-driven going train and two spring-driven, count-wheel striking trains, one striking the hours on a single steel bell on the back plate, the other the quarters on two steel bells also on the back plate. The movement has an anchor escapement and a steel-spring pendulum suspension, replacing an original silk suspension.

The clock belonged to the 4th Marquess of Hertford by 1865, when he lent it to the Musée Rétrospectif exhibition.

F259

Back plate of movement, with pendulum detached

MANTEL CLOCK (*PENDULE DE CHEMINÉE*)

c. 1774

H. 49 cm.(19¼ in.) W. 42 cm.(16½ in.) D. 18 cm.(7³⁄₃₂ in.)

Gilt-bronze case. Movement signed by Jean-André Lepaute (maître 1759, horloger du roi, retired 1774); design of the figures attributed to Étienne-Maurice Falconet (1716–91).

The figures on the clock case show Venus clipping Cupid's wings: Venus has entwined Cupid's body in her drapery, while her right hand, holding the shears, is poised by his left wing. Cupid's torch and quiver lie, one over the other, between his legs. The amorous theme is continued on the relief panel at the front of the base, on which four infants entwine a flaming heart with chains of leaves and flowers, although this presumably illustrates the effects of Cupid's activity before the clipping of his wings. Both Venus and Cupid show analogies with sculptures attributed to Falconet, but the design of the clock can only be tentatively attributed to him, since the clock was certainly made after Falconet's departure for Russia in 1766. This model of clock was evidently made over a period of several years, since an example in the Toledo Museum of Art in Toledo, Ohio, has a movement by Jean-Baptiste Mercier (*maître* 1781).

The clock movement has an eight-day, spring-driven going train and a count-wheel striking train, striking the hours and half-hours on a single bell on the back plate. The movement has a Brocot dead-beat escapement and an adjustable steel-spring pendulum

Back plate of movement

suspension, replacing a silk suspension, formerly adjusted through a hole in the middle of the 60-minute mark.

The clock was probably one of two gilt-bronze clocks inventoried at no. 3 rue Taitbout in August 1871, a year after the death of the 4th Marquess of Hertford.

F261

Mantel Clock (*PENDULE DE CHEMINÉE*)

c. 1775

H. 47 cm.(18½ in.) W. 35.2 cm.(13⅞ in.) D. 27.5 cm.(10⅝ in.)

Gilt-bronze case.
Unsigned movement; design of the case attributed to Étienne-Maurice Falconet (1716–91).

The figures on the clock show the Toilet of Venus, with the goddess sitting at a three-legged table with central baluster stem, while a handmaiden brings her roses and Cupid, who formerly held an arrow in his left hand, indicates the time on the dials which revolve around the table top. The design was attributed by Émile Molinier in about 1900 to Falconet, an attribution which still appears convincing, although the casting and chasing of the clock probably postdate Falconet's departure for Russia in 1766 by a number of years. The head of Venus's handmaiden may be compared to that of Falconet's *Baigneuse* of 1757, as well as to that of his *Douce Mélancolie* of 1763.

The clock movement has an eight-day, spring-driven going train and a count-wheel striking train, striking the hours and half-hours on a steel bell on the back plate. The movement has a platform escapement, which appears to date from the mid-nineteenth century, since the regulator is engraved with both *R* and *A* for *Retard* and *Avance* and *S* and *F* for Slow and Fast. It is not clear with what sort of escapement the clock would originally have been fitted.

The clock belonged to the 4th Marquess of Hertford by 1865, when he lent it to the Musée Rétrospectif exhibition.

F260

Mantel Clock (PENDULE DE CHEMINÉE)

c. 1775

H. 68 cm.(26¾ in.) W. 100.7 cm.(39½ in.) D. 25 cm.(9²⁷⁄₃₂ in.)

Gilt-bronze case, with patinated bronze figures, supported on a Griotte marble base with gilt-bronze feet.
Movement signed Lepaute, *probably for Jean-Baptiste Lepaute (1727–1801); case designed by Antoine-Mathieu Le Carpentier (1709–73).*

The clock follows the design of one made for the gallery of the Palais-Bourbon in Paris and delivered there by Jean-André Lepaute, elder brother of Jean-Baptiste, in 1772. The present clock, which is dated 1775 on its striking spring, must be a slightly later version of the same model, made after Jean-Baptiste Lepaute had taken over his brother's workshop in 1774. The bronze figures of Night and Day are based on the marble figures by Michelangelo on the tomb of Giuliano de' Medici in the New Sacristy of San Lorenzo, Florence. Le Carpentier, who was architect to the prince de Condé at the Palais-Bourbon, was not the first designer to use the Michelangelo figures on a clock design. Night and Day had been used by André-Charles Boulle on a clock design in the early years of the eighteenth century and the models for the

Back plate of movement

bronze figures are listed in his probate inventory in 1732. An example of Boulle's Night and Day model, which survives in the Archives Nationales, was listed in the bedchamber of the duc de Bourbon at Chantilly in 1740; in that year the duke became prince de Condé. When in 1772 the same prince took delivery of the Night and Day clock designed by Le Carpentier, he would have

been aware that the up-to-date neo-classical design was also an updating of a model by André-Charles Boulle.

The movement has an eight-day, spring-driven going train and a count-wheel striking train, striking the hours and half-hours on a bell mounted on the back plate. The movement has a pin-wheel escapement, with an adjusting device for setting the movement in beat, and a steel-spring pendulum suspension, replacing a silk suspension formerly adjusted through a hole above the 60-minute mark. The dial has a blued-steel seconds hand. The striking spring is signed and dated *Richard fevrier 1775* for Claude Richard (recorded in the rue de la Huchette 1754–72).

The clock was inventoried in store at no. 5 rue Taitbout in August 1871, a year after the death of the 4th Marquess of Hertford.

F268

MANTEL CLOCK (*PENDULE DE CHEMINÉE*)

c. 1780

H. 97.1 cm.(38¼ in.) W. 42.2 cm.(16⅝ in.) D. 27.5 cm.(10⁵⁹⁄₆₄ in.)

Case of slate and bronze veneered with lapis lazuli, mounted with gilt bronze and supported on a Griotte marble base; mounted at the front with a gouache medallion on paper.
Movement signed by Jean-Jacques de Lespinasse (still active 1792).

The clock forms a pair with the barometer in the next entry, the theme of the two being the fertility which sun and rain bring to the earth. At the top of the clock case Aurora pushes aside the clouds of darkness to reveal the sun's rays, represented by a radiant disc in her left hand, while between the two banks of cloud the front of the obelisk is mounted with a sundial. The bottom of the obelisk has a trophy of a seed pan, partly encircled by drapery and with leaves and fruit on the right. Ceres, the corn goddess, is seated to the left of the dial, identifiable by the sheaves of corn on which she sits; she looks upwards towards the sun in expectation of harvest time.

The clock case has been altered somewhat in the nineteenth century; the lions' heads at the bottom of the obelisk once fitted more closely against the uprights and the rudder and helm trophy on the front has perhaps been moved from the barometer, where its symbolism would be more appropriate. The infant to the right of Ceres on the base was perhaps formerly mounted at a less extreme angle and may have held an attribute in his left hand.

Gouache medallion from front of case

The clock movement has an eight-day, spring-driven going train and a spring-driven, count-wheel striking train, striking the hours and half-hours on a single bell mounted on the back plate. The movement has an anchor escapement and a steel-spring pendulum suspension with Brocot adjustment, replacing a silk pendulum suspension originally adjusted through a hole above the 60-minute mark. Both the going and striking springs are signed *Richard may 1778* for Claude Richard (recorded in the rue de la Huchette 1754–72).

The clock was inventoried in Hertford House after the death of the 4th Marquess of Hertford in 1870.

F94

Front plate of movement with winding arbors

MANTEL BAROMETER AND THERMOMETER (*BAROMÈTRE ET THERMOMÈTRE DE CHEMINÉE*)

c. 1780

H. 96.8 cm.(38⅛ in.) W. 42.2 cm.(16⅝ in.) D. 27.5 cm.(10⁵⁵⁄₆₄ in.)

Case of slate and bronze veneered with lapis lazuli, mounted with gilt bronze and supported on a Griotte marble base; mounted at the front with a gouache medallion on paper.
Thermometer signed by Scanegatty (recorded 1788); gouache medallion signed on the back Mᵉʳ ᴰᴱ BARBAREY Fect 1854.

The barometer forms a pair with the clock in the preceding entry, the figures on the barometer referring to rainfall, rather than to sunshine. At the top of the obelisk is Iris, emptying a pitcher held under her right arm and parting two banks of cloud with her left hand. The corners of the obelisk rest on dolphins' heads, in place of the lions' heads on the clock, and Neptune is seated on the base, with his right arm on top of the barometer dial. A gilt-bronze basket of flowers and fruit at the front of the obelisk is again symbolic of fruitfulness. The combination of Neptune on the barometer with Ceres on the clock is appropriate, not merely because of the theme of water in the decoration of the barometer, but because in Greek mythology Demeter (Ceres) sometimes appears as the consort of Poseidon (Neptune) in his capacity of earth-holder or husband of Earth.

Like the matching clock, the barometer case has been altered in the nineteenth century. The dolphins' heads formerly fitted more tightly against the corners of the obelisk and the Cupid on the base has been moved and would originally have had his torch with him, rather than at the other side of the base. The date of these alterations was perhaps that recorded on the back of the gouache medallion.

Above, gouache medallion from front of case.
Left, detail of thermometer

The thermometer on the front of the obelisk is graduated in degrees Réaumur from minus 3 to 45; the thermometer plate is engraved *Paris 1753* by the 30-degree mark, but this records an exceptional temperature, not the date of the thermometer itself.

The barometer was inventoried in Hertford House after the death of the 4th Marquess of Hertford in 1870.

F95

MANTEL CLOCK (*PENDULE DE CHEMINÉE*)

c. 1780

H. 62.5 cm.(24⅝ in.) W. 35 cm.(13¾ in.) D. 25 cm.(9²⁷⁄₃₂ in.)

Case of gilt, patinated and enamelled bronze, supported on a porphyry plinth. Unsigned movement; case attributed to Étienne Martincourt (maître 1762), working to a design by Augustin Pajou (1730–1809).

The clock represents the theme of Love Triumphing over Time, though in a more elaborate form than that designed by André-Charles Boulle. Time has been tied up with a long wreath of flowers, one end of which is held by Love, who also holds up an arrow in his left hand to indicate the time on the dials which revolve round the globe. Time's right arm rests on the globe, with the right hand still cupped where it held his hour glass, which has been seized by another winged infant to the upper left of the globe. Behind Time, a third winged infant, hovering below Time's left wing, seizes the other end of the scythe handle. A much larger version of the same model of clock was attributed to Martincourt and Pajou in the sale of the gilder Pierre-François Feuchère in 1824. The larger version had been made in about 1780–1 for the duchesse de Mazarin, but had been left with the musical box in its base unfinished at her death in 1781. The present clock may thus be dated c. 1780; it would have been cast by Martincourt, who was a bronze founder, but a sculptural model for the design, in terracotta or some similar material, would have been provided by the sculptor, Pajou.

Back plate of movement

The clock movement has an eight-day, spring-driven going train and a spring-driven, count-wheel striking train, striking the hours and half-hours on a bell mounted at the back of the movement. The movement has an anchor escapement and a silk pendulum suspension and is mounted with the back plate and the pendulum facing towards the front of the case.

The clock was bought by the 4th Marquess of Hertford at the sale of his half-brother, Lord Henry Seymour, held in Paris in February 1860.

F264

Right side of case

Long-case Clock (*Régulateur*)

c. 1780

H. 221.2 cm.(87 in.) W. 56.8 cm.(22⅜ in.) D. 34.5 cm.(13⅝ in.)

Case of oak and pinewood, veneered with tulipwood and satiné,
with gilt-bronze mounts.
Movement signed by Jacques-Joseph Lepaute, called Lepaute de Bellefontaine
(maître *1775); case stamped by Nicolas Petit (1732–91, maître 1761).*

The clock dates from c. 1780, but incorporates the chariot of Apollo mount on top, which is of earlier design. The mount illustrates Ovid, *Metamorphoses*, II, 153–5, showing the chariot of the sun god just before its departure across the sky. It is of the same model as that on top of the long-case clock in the Frick Collection, which bears the engraved inscription: *Les Bronze* (sic) *Par Caffiéri L'ainé 1767*, and which otherwise resembles the other Wallace Collection long-case clock (pp. 56–7), which has therefore been dated c. 1768. The present clock, on the other hand, has a movement by a clockmaker who

**Detail of dial and
compensating pendulum**

only became a *maître* in 1775, clearly dates from at least six years after Philippe Caffiéri's death and combines the chariot of Apollo with other mounts that have none of the weighty, early neo-classical character of those on the Frick clock. The likelihood of Philippe Caffiéri having cast the group on the present clock seems remote, since such an expensive casting would hardly have been left unused for a number of years. It is more likely that the Apollo group was cast c. 1780 especially for the present clock, but using a model of c. 1767, possibly preserved by the sculptor who made the original design and who cannot therefore have been Caffiéri. Other

clock cases by Petit are similarly treated to this one, being used as plinths to support pieces of sculpture or scientific instruments. A long-case clock of this type, acquired in Paris by Gouverneur Morris in about 1792, is surmounted by a bronze bust of Cicero, which bears no relation to the other mounts.

The clock movement has an eight-day, weight-driven going train, with the weight suspended from a spiked brass pulley on a Huygens endless cord. The movement has a pin-wheel escapement and a compensating pendulum made up of five steel and four brass rods; the pendulum has a steel-spring suspension. There is no striking train and the going train is wound by pulling the Huygens cord manually. The dial has a blued steel seconds hand and a blued steel pointer for the day of the month.

The clock was probably one of four long-case clocks inventoried together at no. 2 rue Laffitte in August 1871, a year after the death of the 4th Marquess of Hertford.

F270

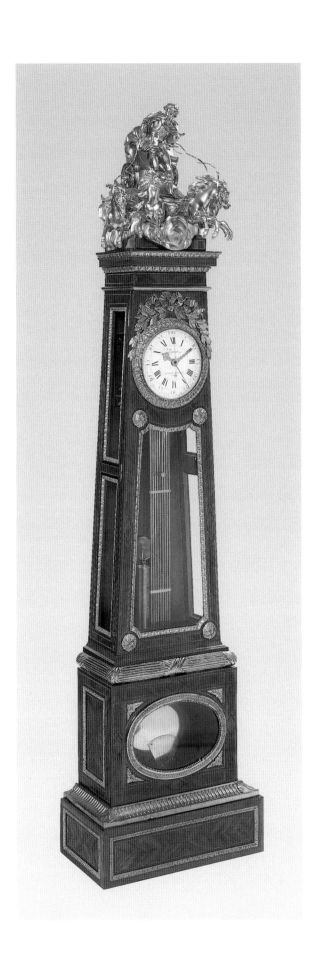

MANTEL CLOCK (*PENDULE DE CHEMINÉE*)

c. 1781

H. 53 cm.(20⅞ in.) W. 56 cm.(22 in.) D. 18 cm.(7⅜ in.)

Gilt-bronze case supported on a stone base, painted to resemble verde antico *marble. Movement signed by Jean-Baptiste Lepaute (1727–1801, maître 1776) and dated 1781, with enamel dial signed* G Merlet *(enameller recorded in 1812); design of the case attributed to François-Joseph Belanger (1744–1818).*

The date 1781 scratched on the dial plate may be taken as the date of the whole clock, which is closely related to a clock supplied by Lepaute in that year to the comte d'Artois, for the *salon* of the château of Bagatelle. The present clock is not to be identified with the one for Bagatelle, on which the sphinxes were richly draped and which was supported on eight feet rather than six. The Bagatelle clock was based on a design by Belanger, architect of the little château, and was intended to stand on the salon chimneypiece, carved by Augustin Bocciardi and mounted with a gilt-bronze interlace frieze probably chased and gilded by Gouthière. The interlace on the chimneypiece was not unlike that on the base of the present clock, though without the signs of the Zodiac, so that the base of the present clock may have borne a general resemblance to that of the Bagatelle one. Lepaute also noted on his bill to the comte d'Artois that a similar clock had been supplied to the comte de Provence. The sphinxes on these clocks seem to represent a transition between the winged female sphinx, deriving from Greek art, and the wingless, male Egyptian sphinx.

The clock movement has an eight-day, spring-driven

Back of case

going train and a count-wheel striking train, striking the hours and half-hours on a bell mounted on the back plate. The movement has a pin-wheel escapement and a silk pendulum suspension.

The clock was probably one of two clocks, described as Empire, inventoried together at no. 5 rue Taitbout, Paris in August 1871, a year after the death of the 4th Marquess of Hertford.

F269

CLOCK AND CANDELABRUM (*PENDULE ET CANDÉLABRE*)

c. 1781

H. 224.2 cm.(88⅛ in.) W. 45 cm.(17¾ in.) D.45.2 cm.(17¾ in.)

Case of gilt bronze and of white, verde antico *and Griotte marble, mounted with a patinated bronze figure.*
Unsigned movement; design of the case attributed to Étienne-Maurice Falconet (1716–91).

The clock is dominated by the bronze figure of Cupid, who tramples on two gilt-bronze books and encircles the sheaf of candelabrum branches with his left arm. The use of stems of poppies, the source of opiates, as the candle branches, implies that the clock was made for a bedchamber, in which the presence of Cupid would also have been appropriate. A screw hole in Cupid's left breast and another in his upper left arm show that a further attribute, possibly a bow or an arrow, is missing. Cupid can be described as in the style of Falconet and certainly reflects the influence of Falconet's *Baigneuse* of 1757, but the attribution must remain tentative, as Falconet was in St Petersburg from 1766 to 1778 and did not return to Paris until November 1780.

The rotating dials, of gilt brass, are mounted at the top of the white marble vase, where the time is indicated by the tongue of a gilt-bronze serpent entwined round the neck of the vase. The movement itself is mounted in the cylindrical pedestal supporting Cupid, so that the arbor driving the dials has to be very long indeed. The Griotte marble plinth below the cylindrical pedestal was probably added in the nineteenth century.

The movement has an eight-day, spring-driven going train and a spring-driven, rack striking train, striking the hours and half-hours on a steel bell on the back plate. The movement has a Brocot dead-beat escapement, with agate pallet stones, and a steel-spring pendulum suspension. The going and striking trains are wound through two brass-lined apertures on the right of the cylindrical pedestal.

The clock was bought for the 4th Marquess of Hertford on the fourteenth day of the Stowe sale, 1 September 1848.

F272

CLOCK VASE AND COVER (*VASE 'PENDULE BOIZOT'*)

c. 1781

H. 44.4 cm.(17½ in.) W. 22.1 cm.(8¹⁵⁄₆₄ in.)

Hard-paste Sèvres porcelain vase, decorated with a pale green pointillé *ground, with gilding on the relief decoration, supported on a gilt-bronze stand enclosing four hard-paste Sèvres porcelain plaques.*
Movement signed L. Montjoye A Paris, *either for Louis Montjoye (maître 1748) or for his son Jean-Louis Montjoye (maître 1766); vase designed by Louis-Simon Boizot (1743–1809).*

The vase *'pendule Boizot'* was first recorded at the Sèvres factory in June–August 1781, when a sculptor named Chanou was still working on the master model. Once that was complete, the vase appears to have been put into production. On 22 November 1781 the painter Vincent Taillandier (1736–90) applied *pointillé* grounds to two examples, one of which may have been the present vase; the same two vases were gilded by Étienne-Henry Le Guay (1719/20–c. 1799) before the final firing on 12 December 1781. The infant terms at the corners of the vase are similar to those used by Boizot in 1771–2 on a marble and gilt-bronze chimneypiece, with mounts chased and gilded by Pierre Gouthière, for Madame du Barry's *salon* in the Garden of Diana at Fontainebleau. The chimneypiece was moved under Louis XVI to his private library at Versailles, where it remains. As well as an aperture at the front, filled by the clock dial, the vase also has one at the back, filled by a hinged gilt-bronze door, and raised roundels at the sides, overlaid with gilt-bronze trophies.

The clock movement has an eight-day, spring-driven going train and a spring-driven, count-wheel striking train, striking the hours and half-hours on a steel bell mounted on the back plate.

The movement has an anchor escapement and a silk pendulum suspension, adjusted through a hole in the dial plate just above the 60-minute mark.

The clock vase belonged to the 4th Marquess of Hertford by 1865, when he lent it to the Musée Rétrospectif exhibition.

C337

Back plate of movement

MANTEL CLOCK (*PENDULE DE CHEMINÉE*)

c. 1785

H. 60.5 cm.(23⅞ in.) W. 39 cm.(15⅜ in.) D. 22 cm.(8²¹⁄₃₂ in.)

Case of gilt and enamelled bronze.
Movement signed by Robert Robin (1742–99, maître *1767,* valet de chambre, *horloger de la Reine 1786); enamelled band round the vase signed by Joseph Coteau (1740–1812).*

The clock is closely related to one supplied by Robin for Marie-Antoinette at Saint-Cloud, but cannot be the Queen's clock, on which the infants represented the arts, those on the present clock holding attributes of Astronomy and Geometry. Both clocks no doubt had the crowing

cock on the right, representing the wakefulness essential for successful study, and both were probably made after February 1785, when the château of Saint-Cloud was acquired by Louis XVI. The truncated column on the Wallace Collection clock and the vase it supports are both enamelled blue, but the colour has probably darkened with time; the column on the Saint-Cloud example was described by Robin as being '*en faux lapis*', in other words as resembling lapis lazuli. The enamelled band on the vase of the present clock, which is signed by Joseph Coteau and can be revolved manually, is painted with grisaille panels set in simulated stone surrounds showing infants representing the seasons. The shallow compositions, imitating sculpture, are reminiscent of the grisaille overdoors which Piat Sauvage painted for so many rooms at Fontainebleau and Compiègne in the 1780s. On the clock the grisaille seasons are separated by profile antique heads, also in grisaille, but reserved against black backgrounds within oval gilt frames against panels of simulated lapis lazuli.

Above, back of clock case.
Left, detail of band on vase with signature of Coteau on left-hand side, and infants representing Summer

The movement has an eight-day, spring-driven going train and a spring-driven, count-wheel striking train, striking the hours and half-hours on a bell on the back plate. The movement has an anchor escapement and a silk pendulum suspension, adjusted through a hole in the dial plate by the 10-minute mark. The winding arbors are at the bottom of the movement; when a knob below the front of the plinth is pressed, the front gilt-bronze panel springs open, giving access to them.

The clock belonged in the mid-nineteenth century to Prince Anatole Demidoff at the Palazzo San Donato, Florence, and was bought by Mannheim for the 4th Marquess of Hertford at the San Donato sale in Paris in March 1870.

F263

Mantel Clock *(pendule de cheminée)*

c. 1785

H. 30.7 cm.(12³⁄₃₂ in.) W. 18.9 cm.(7⁷⁄₁₆ in.) D. 10.2 cm.(4¹⁄₆₄ in.)

Gilt-bronze case, mounted with nine hard-paste porcelain plaques.
Movement signed by Jean-Baptiste-François Cronier (maître 1781), with enamel dial signed
by Pierre Bezelle (recorded 1768).

In shape the clock res-
embles a miniature version
of a Louis XVI drop-front
secretaire, with a raised
gallery round the top,
three tiers of panels at the
sides and a wider base with
bracket feet. The porcelain
plaques have been identi-
fied as late eighteenth-
century imitations of
Sèvres porcelain, probably
made in Paris. The round
plaque on the right side is marked with interlaced Ls
in underglaze blue and with the mark of the Sèvres
painter, Jean-Baptiste Tandart, both probably fake;
the faking of Sèvres marks appears to have already
been practised in the eighteenth century. The plaques
on the clock are certainly imitating Sèvres *plaques 'de
pendule'*, introduced in 1773, but they have been
chamfered at the edges and filed at the corners;
co-ordination between the minor porcelain factory
and the shopkeeper who probably commissioned the
clock was by no means as good as would have been
the case between the Sèvres porcelain factory and a
major *marchand-mercier* like Dominique Daguerre.

The clock movement has an eight-day, spring-driven
going train and a spring-driven, count-wheel striking
train, striking the hours and half-hours on a steel bell
mounted on the back plate. The movement has

**The nine porcelain plaques
from the case, unmounted**

an anchor escapement and
a silk pendulum suspen-
sion, adjusted through a
hole in the middle of the
60-minute mark.

The clock belonged to the
4th Marquess of Hertford
by 1865, when he lent it to
the Musée Rétrospectif exhibition in Paris.

F265

Column Clock (*pendule à colonne*)

c. 1786

H. 35.7 cm.(14 in.) Diam. of base 17.3 cm.(6¹³⁄₁₆ in.)

Sèvres soft-paste porcelain column, mounted with gilt bronze on a white marble base and
supporting a Sèvres soft-paste porcelain vase.
*Movement signed by Germain Dubois (*maître *1757,* horloger de Mesdames*); vase marked with the date*
letters for 1786, column with the gilder's mark of Michel-Barnabé Chauvaux (b. 1730, active 1752–88).

The porcelain column, in which the clock movement is inserted, was known at the Sèvres factory as a *colonne 'à pendule'*, a model first listed in 1772, but in fact already in production in 1771. The vase on top, of a model first identifiable in August 1778, was known as a *petit vase pour la colonne à pendule*. The present clock is thus a late example of this model, although the column was still available at the factory in 1791. The *marchand-mercier* Simon-Philippe Poirier was probably responsible for the introduction of the *colonne 'à pendule'*, which is found with two different sets of gilt-bronze mounts, the second set having the column flanked by gilt-bronze figures of Love and Friendship, represented by a female figure holding two hearts in her outstretched hand and by an infant playing with a dog. A further variation is that columns with mounts like those on the present clock are also found on gilt-bronze platforms with marble obelisks on either side and with biscuit porcelain figures of Falconet's *La Baigneuse* and Gillet's *Le Berger Paris* in front of the obelisks. The earliest documented example of the *colonne 'à pendule'*, sold by Poirier to Madame du Barry in December 1771, was probably mounted in this way.

The clock movement has an eight-day, spring-driven going train and a count-wheel striking train, striking the hours and half-hours on a bell mounted on the back plate. The movement has an anchor escapement and a silk pendulum suspension, adjusted through a hole occupying the 60-minute position on the dial.

The movement is supported on a brass rod attached to the gilt-bronze collars below the column.

The column clock belonged to the 4th Marquess of Hertford by 1865, when he lent it to the Musée Rétrospectif exhibition.

F262

GLOSSARY

Anchor escapement: an escapement with the pallets in the form of an inverted anchor, in which the pallets push the escape wheel slightly backwards at the end of each swing; also called a recoil escapement.

Aneroid barometer: a barometer which dispenses with the use of liquid, i.e. mercury, by using a vacuum chamber on a spring to measure atmospheric pressure.

Arbor: a spindle or shaft, on which a rotating wheel or lever is mounted.

Barometer: an instrument for measuring atmospheric pressure.

Bleu turquin marble: grey marble with a blueish tinge.

Blued steel: steel given a blue colour by being heated.

Brocot adjustment: a screw-threaded adjustment for a steel-spring suspension invented by Achille Brocot (1817–74).

Brocot escapement: a type of semi-dead-beat escapement patented by Louis-Gabriel Brocot in 1840.

Cam: an eccentric projection on a revolving shaft, shaped so as to give linear motion to another part.

Carillon: a mechanism for playing tunes on a set of bells.

Cartel: a wall-clock shaped like a decorative cartouche.

Centre seconds hand: a seconds hand which moves round the circumference of a clock dial, rather than round a smaller inset dial.

Chapter ring: the ring on the dial on which the numbers are painted or engraved.

Chronometer: an instrument for the accurate measurement of time.

Compensating pendulum: a pendulum constructed so as to counteract the expansion and contraction of metal under variations of temperature.

Contre-partie marquetry: Boulle marquetry of brass and tortoiseshell, with the brass used for the background and the tortoiseshell for the design.

Dead-beat escapement: an escapement resembling an anchor escapement in which part of the pallets are formed from an arc of a circle with the pallet arbor as its centre, so as to avoid any recoil on the escape wheel.

Equation of time: the difference between apparent solar time, as told by a sundial, and mean time, as told by an accurate, uniform clock.

Equation kidney: a kidney-shaped cam which, by acting on a solar time hand on a clock dial, can convert mean time into apparent solar time.

Escapement: the part of a timepiece that checks the driving force and prevents it from running down without interruption.

Escape wheel: the toothed wheel on which the escapement pallets act.

Fusee: a cone-shaped spindle on which is wound a chain driven by the spring barrel, in order to produce a uniform driving force.

Going train: that part of the wheelwork in a clock which is concerned with keeping time.

Grid-iron pendulum: a pendulum constructed as a framework of metal bars, in order to compensate for different temperatures.

Griotte marble: a dark-red marble from the Pyrenees.

Grisaille: a painting in greyish tints in imitation of bas-reliefs.

Huygens endless cord: a cord whose ends are joined together to form a continuous loop, used for suspending the weight in a clock; named after Christian Huygens (1629–95).

Knife-edge suspension: a sharp piece of steel serving as the axis of balance for the top of a pendulum.

Lapis lazuli: a stone consisting of calcite coloured ultramarine.

Long-case clock: a weight-driven clock, generally with a long pendulum, in a tall case.

Mean time: an average throughout the year of time by the Sun, but going, unlike apparent solar time, at a constant rate.

Mercuric barometer: a barometer measuring atmospheric pressure by the rise and fall of mercury in a glass tube open at one end.

Movement: the mechanism of a clock or watch.

Pallet: the surface or part of an escapement on which the teeth of the escape wheel act to give impulse to the escapement.

Pendulum: a swinging weight used for regulating the movement of a clock.

Pin-wheel escapement: in which the arms of an anchor or gate embrace either side of a series of pins mounted on the face of the escape wheel.

Planisphere: a sphere projected on a plane.

Platform escapement: an escapement using a balance wheel with a balance spring, instead of a pendulum.

Porphyry: a hard, variegated rock, of a purple and white colour, quarried by the Romans in Upper Egypt.

Première-partie marquetry: Boulle marquetry of brass and tortoiseshell, with the tortoiseshell used for the background and the brass for the design.

Rack striking: a striking system controlled by a snail-shaped piece acting with a toothed rack which is gathered up, one tooth for each blow struck, by a gathering pallet.

Réaumur scale: a thermometer scale invented by R.-A.-F. de Réaumur (1683–1757), having the freezing point of water at 0° and the boiling point at 80°.

Recoil: the backwards push given to the escape wheel by the pallets of the verge and anchor escapements.

Repeat: a mechanism by which a clock can be made to strike the last hour, quarter, etc., when required.

Satiné: a dark-red hardwood imported into France from Brazil and Guyana.

Silk suspension: in which the top of the pendulum is suspended from a loop of thread wound round an arbor at the top of the movement.

Solar time: apparent solar time, as read off a sundial; it is not constant, because of the Earth's elliptical orbit round the sun and because of the angle at which it rotates.

Spring-driven movement: a movement with the driving force provided by the unwinding of a coiled steel spring.

FOR FURTHER READING

Train: any series of wheels in a clock movement.

Verge escapement: the earliest type of escapement, in which the teeth at the top and bottom of the crown wheel engage the pallets at the top and bottom of a shaft (verge), which is turned first one way and then the other.

Weight-driven movement: a movement with the driving force provided by the pull of a weight suspended on a cord or chain.

Baulez, C., 'La Pendule A La Geoffrin', *L'Estampille/L'Objet D'Art*, 224, April 1989, pp. 34–41.

Bellaigue, G. de, *The James A. De Rothschild Collection At Waddesdon Manor: Furniture, Clocks And Gilt Bronzes*, London, 1974.

Dell, T., 'The Gilt-bronze Cartel Clocks of Charles Cressent', *The Burlington Magazine*, CIX, 1967, pp. 210–17.

Dubon, D. and Dell, T., *The Frick Collection, V, Furniture In The Frick Collection*, New York, 1992.

Edey, W., *French Clocks in North American Collections*, exhibition catalogue, The Frick Collection, New York, 1982.

Eriksen, S., *Early Neo-Classicism in France*, London, 1974.

Hawley, H., 'Jean-Pierre Latz, Cabinetmaker', *Bulletin of The Cleveland Museum of Art*, September/October 1970, pp. 203–59.

Hughes, P., 'Heavenly Timepiece', *Country Life*, April 23 1992, pp. 54–5.

Ottomeyer, H. and Pröschel, P., *Vergoldete Bronzen*, Munich, 1986.

Ronfort, J.-N. and Augarde, J.-D., 'Le Maître Du Bureau De L'Electeur', *L'Estampille/L'Objet D'Art*, 243, January 1991, pp. 42–75.

Savill, R., *The Wallace Collection, Catalogue of Sèvres Porcelain*, London, 1988.

Tait, H., *Clocks and Watches*, The British Museum, London, 1983.

Tardy, *Dictionnaire Des Horlogers Français*, Paris, 1971–2.

Verlet, P., *Les Bronzes Dorés Français du xviiie siècle*, Paris, 1987.

Watson, F. J. B., *Wallace Collection Catalogues, Furniture*, London, 1956.

Wilson, G., *French Eighteenth-Century Clocks In The J. Paul Getty Museum*, Malibu, 1976.

INDEX OF NAMES AND PLACES

ACKNOWLEDGEMENTS

We wish to extend our thanks to Job Parilux, Toulouse, for generously sponsoring the paper for this book.

PHOTOGRAPHIC ACKNOWLEDGEMENTS

We should like to thank the following for making copyright photographs available:

The J. Paul Getty Museum, Malibu:
Venus Marina, French bronze c. 1710, page 20

Réunion des Musées Nationaux, Paris:
André-Charles Boulle (1642–1732). Bracket clock, with the Three Fates as on the drop front of F413, Musée du Louvre, Paris, OA 11029, page 22

Musée des Arts Décoratifs, Paris:
André-Charles Boulle (1642–1732). Drawing for the clock case of a wardrobe clock, page 24
André-Charles Boulle (1642–1732). Design for a clock representing Love Triumphing over Time, page 30

VALE

P.